A few reviews of Mary Jane

★ ★ ★ ★ ★

"Read one of New Zealand author Mary Jane Walker's informed and richly entertaining travel books and the thirst for more adventures leads to searching for additional volumes."

Grady Harp, Amazon Hall of Fame reviewer, from a review of *A Maverick Traveller Anthology*, 20 April 2019

★ ★ ★ ★ ★

'Do take a walk with Mary Jane Walker!'

"In the tradition of Gertrude Bell, Freya Stark, Isabella Bird and other adventurous women, Mary Jane Walker's relationship with the world is one of insatiable curiosity. She is driven to immerse herself in experience. I was happy to walk with Walker around the world, and was pulled in by her prose."

Brooklyn Stooptalk, from an Amazon review of *A Maverick Traveller*, 20 April 2018

★ ★ ★ ★ ★

'Marvellous Information!!!!'

"Just an enriching book on a place I knew very little about. I've always said that the purpose of reading is acquiring new knowledge & I did!"

D. West, from an Amazon review of *A Maverick New Zealand Way*, 22 May 2019

★ ★ ★ ★

'An Interesting Travel Memoir'

From a review of *A Maverick Himalayan Way,* new edition, by 'Piaras', Amazon Vine Voice reviewer, 24 May 2019

… and a further testimonial

"Hey. We met for 9 years in Russia. You told me about your travels, and then I had not yet visited other countries. Now, thanks to you, I have visited 27 countries. Thanks."

Matvei Ogulov, Russian musician, in a recent Facebook message (2020).

See all Mary Jane's books and blog on a-maverick.com

THE NEGLECTED NORTH ISLAND
New Zealand's other half

An expanded and updated version of the first part of the 2018 award finalist, *A Maverick New Zealand Way.*

TRAVELLER

MARY JANE WALKER

A MAVERICK NEW ZEALAND WAY

INTERNATIONAL BOOK AWARDS FINALIST

IntlBookAwards.com

Mary Jane Walker

Mary Jane Walker is a writer of historically well-informed travel narratives that come with an autobiographical flavour. Born in the North Island town of Hastings, Mary Jane describes eight tours around the island of her birth in this book.

So, travel with Mary Jane around the North Island, an island often neglected in the standard tourism images of New Zealand, which focus on the South Island.

The North Island is the island with volcanoes, mud pools and more Māori culture than the South Island. It also contains New Zealand's biggest cities and lushest forests. And Hobbiton!

Facebook: facebook.com/amavericktraveller
Instagram: @a_maverick_traveller
Twitter: @Mavericktravel0
Email: maryjanewalker@a-maverick.com
Linkedin: Mary Jane Walker

First published 2020 by Mary Jane Walker

A Maverick Traveller Ltd.

PO BOX 44 146, Point Chevalier, Auckland 1246

a-maverick.com

ISBN-13: 978-0-473-52908-6 (paperback), 978-0-473-52910-9 (Kindle), 978-0-473-52909-3 (other epubs)

Disclaimer

This book is a travel memoir, not an outdoors guide. Although the author and publisher have made every effort to ensure that the information in this book was correct at the time of publication, the author and publisher do not assume and hereby disclaim any liability to any party for any loss, damage, or disruption caused by errors or omissions, whether such errors or omissions result from negligence, accident, or any other cause. Some names have also been changed to disguise and protect certain individuals.

Notes on Image Sources All maps and aerial views are credited with the original source. Abbreviations which may be used in image credits or otherwise are as follows:

DOC: New Zealand Department of Conservation
LINZ: Land Information New Zealand

Contents

The North Island of New Zealand. *Source: detail from the NASA Earth Observatory image 2010/099. Insert: Pōhutukawa, common on coasts north of the latitude of Mount Taranaki, and symbolic of Christmas and warm summers.*

The North Island in relation to the other main islands of New Zealand. *The map shown is based on NASA Earth Observatory image 2010/099.*

Notes on Maps and Images

If you have a copy of this book in which the images are printed in black and white, or if you have a Kindle with a black-and-white screen, you can see all of the images in this book that were originally in colour in full colour, and all of the images including chapter-specific maps generally at higher resolution, by going to the blog posts linked at the end of each chapter.

In fact, these blog posts will generally contain more images than appear in the book.

The maps that appear in this book have been drawn from a variety of sources, including two key government agencies, the New Zealand Department of Conservation (DOC) and Land Information New Zealand (LINZ).

Unless noted or indicated otherwise, all maps, aerial photos and satellite images are shown with north at the top.

Readers are in every case urged to make use of original maps (often zoomable if online) and guides when in the outdoors; the maps and aerial/satellite images shown in this book are purely for illustration.

For a literally more all-round perspective, you might also wish to look at some of localities I describe in the 3D view on Google Earth.

Introduction: why miss out on Māui's Fish?

THERE'S a joke map of New Zealand that labels the southwestern tip of the South Island as "The Part where all the Tourist Photos Come From."

Many a true word is spoken in jest. The southwestern tip of the country really *is* the part where most of the tourist photos come from, at any rate. Photos like this one.

And that's fair enough up to a point. Yet there is plenty more to the country to be seen. In particular, the whole of the North

Island is just about completely neglected by travellers and tourists, who thus miss out on the country's Māori culture for one thing: a culture generally less conspicuous in the southern part of the country, where there are fewer Māori and where most towns have English or Scottish names.

In fact, much of the South Island is really quite similar to somewhere that you could visit in the Northern Hemisphere, thus avoiding the lengthy plane journey.

Its two major cities of Christchurch and Dunedin are closely modelled on the stone boroughs of England and Scotland respectively. That gives those cities a lot of charm. But even so, you could be fooled into thinking that you are not actually in New Zealand but rather in Shropshire or Perthshire.

The South Island's mountain scenes are scenic to be sure. But also, in most places, it's scenery of the sort that could be seen on any continent.

Queenstown, the country's greatest tourist trap and gateway to several skifields, seems to me like a cross between Norway and Lake Como with American trees.

Pines and redwoods were planted there to make up for the fact that few New Zealand trees flourished in such a bleak spot. Willows were added along the lakeshore and rose gardens as well. The result is very pretty these days. But none of it is unique to New Zealand.

Which is not to say that the North Island doesn't have plenty of scenery of its own. As the rear cover of this book suggests, in many places the North Island's a subtropical paradise of green Pacific jungles and beaches.

A few years ago, I wrote a book called *A Maverick New Zealand Way*. But later one, I began to think that I'd been seduced by the wonders of the South Island, myself, and hadn't given the North Island enough coverage.

And so, I have written this book in an attempt to even up the inter-island score. To make the bold claim that the North Island is perhaps the real New Zealand. And in any case to overcome the unreasonable neglect of the North Island, an island often likened in its outline by the Māori to a stingray, and thus known as Te Ika a Māui, or Māui's Fish.

This book is framed in terms of eight road tours that you can do, starting from the north. These tours are:

Tour 1: The Tail of the Fish (including Auckland)
Tour 2: Coromandel, the Bay of Plenty and East Cape
Tour 3: The Historic Waikato
Tour 4: The Volcanic Desert, the Thermal Region and
Tour 5: Hawkes Bay and the Wairarapa
Tour 6: Wild, Weird, Windy Wellington
Tour 7: The Manawatu, Whanganui City and Taranaki
Tour 8: The Whanganui River, Pureora, and the Forgotten World

Chapter 1 is a chapter of travel tips.

Chapters 2 to 33 are all about specific places on the eight tours. They also mention useful local websites and apps if there are any or if they haven't been mentioned, already, in the last chapter or two.

The roads in the tours are mostly main roads: if you are riding a bicycle it makes sense to plan your route in ways that might take you off the main roads, for instance by taking advantage of any cycle trails that might be nearby.

Each of these chapters links, at its end, to one or more blog posts that contain additional information, usually in the form of more pictures than I could fit into this book! Some have other notes as well.

The final chapter, Chapter 34, Te Araroa, describes New Zealand's 'Long Trail', which runs through both islands, has a website of its own, and passes through many scenic destinations, each of which is accessible to the last one, and the next one, on foot or by mountain bike.

CHAPTER ONE

Travel Tips

SAVE for the yellow-bellied sea snake that occasionally drifts down from Fiji, we New Zealanders don't have any snakes. Nor do we have crocodiles, venomous ticks or cassowaries to kick you to death. And you aren't too likely to die of thirst either.

Such are the differences between New Zealand and Australia, which at first glance make New Zealand seem a cosy sort of a place.

All the same, outdoor New Zealand, where the terrain is steep and where it rains a lot, isn't without its hazards of mountains, water and bad weather.

So, in this travel tips chapter, I'll start with a note on outdoor safety. This will be followed by a description of the best places to get maps and travel brochures, a section on camping information, and a section on some other useful apps.

At the end of this chapter, I'll link to a blog post of mine that has more travel tips than I could fit in here.

Outdoor Safety First

In this photograph from the rear cover, I'm wading through some fairly deep water: which is a common thing to have to do if you're outdoorsy enough in New Zealand.

But if you look closely you can see my legs and feet and the bottom I'm standing on. In other words, the water is clear and any hazards like rocks or logs can be seen. And the water's also not going anywhere very fast either. Avoiding muddy, swift water is a good habit to learn for surviving in our land of rivers, beaches and lakes.

It's also important to have access to warm and waterproof clothing even in summer, follow the weather forecasts and assume that the weather might get worse anyway.

And, to read officially-approved maps and leaflets about the areas that you are planning to visit. These contain relevant safety information.

Studying the relevant information also means that you are less likely to miss out on something worth seeing, as well.

Last but not least, beware of Kiwi drivers and always keep left!

Visitor Centres, i-Sites and Topo Maps

To get reliable and up-to-date information about the outdoors in New Zealand, the first place to go, either physically or online, is the New Zealand Department of Conservation (DOC), which has many Visitor Centres around the country plus a website, **doc.govt.nz**.

Many of New Zealand's outdoor destinations are described in a page on the DOC website or in a PDF brochure you can download from it, or both. You can pick up the brochures in paper form from DOC or from other distributors such as the i-Sites (below). And all DOC information is free.

For other tourist destinations, including the cities, an equivalent one-stop wealth of information is provided by the national i-Site system, the 'i-' standing for 'information'. The i-Sites are run by a government agency called Tourism New Zealand, and their website is **isite.nz**.

Sometimes DOC and the i-Sites share the same premises. On the next page there's a photo of DOC's Tongariro National Park Visitor Centre, which also has i-Site signs outside it.

Source: Ruapehu District Council

Detailed topographical maps are provided by Land Information New Zealand (LINZ), and you can buy these in paper form from various book shops, i-Sites and DOC Visitor Centres, or access them electronically. A free, zoomable site is NZ Topo Map, on **topomap.co.nz**. There is also no shortage of New Zealand topographical map apps on the Apple and Google Play stores.

Camping Information

There's endless political argument in New Zealand about toilet waste left behind by freedom campers (i.e., casual campers). For some reason it seems easier for politicians to argue about the issue rather than spring for the cost of building more public toilets at popular beauty spots.

A frequent result is the posting of the rather Orwellian message 'Freedom Camping Forbidden', or words to that effect. And even if you just lay up on the side of the road for a few hours it probably won't be long before some hypervigilant farmer turns up to shoo you away, even though it's the government's policy that it's better to rest than keep driving if you're tired.

At any rate, if you are a camper or a person in a van it's vital to know where you can camp: knowledge that also helps with planning undisturbed rest breaks.

There's a website that addresses the issue. It's called Camping in New Zealand and its website address is **freedomcamping.org**. The website links to two apps, the CampingNZ app and the CamperMate app.

Some other useful web resources and apps

100% Pure New Zealand (website **newzealand.com**). It doesn't get more high-level than that! The New Zealand Government's window on the world. Hit the Travel button if your interest is travel, as opposed to Invest, Study, or Live&Work.

MetService (website **metservice.com**, and app). Your go-to site and app for New Zealand official weather updates.

Star Chart (app). The constellations in the Southern Hemisphere are completely different to the ones in the North, the Milky Way is more impressive down here, and on top of that, New Zealand has many areas with really dark skies. Two out of the world's thirteen Dark Sky Sanctuaries are in New Zealand, one of them less than ninety kilometres from the big city of Auckland on Aotea / Great Barrier Island. All of the others are in places that are extremely remote, including New Zealand's other Dark Sky Sanctuary at Rakiura / Stewart Island. Many other places in New Zealand are quite dark at night as well, so give it a go!

Tramping, Tracks and Trails

Oh, a couple of last things about the peculiarities of New Zealand English as it applies to the outdoors. You'll come across the word 'tramping' many times in this book. This is the New Zealand word for what the British call hiking and the Australians bushwalking. And likewise, the verb to tramp, meaning to hike or bushwalk. On the other hand, the noun 'tramp' still has the same meaning as in Britain. So, in New Zealand, hikers and bushwalkers are called trampers, never tramps!

As for the trails that people tramp, hike or bushwalk along, they tend to be called 'tracks' rather than trails if they are too rugged for cyclists. In today's outdoor New Zealand the word 'trail' has a sort of semi-domesticated significance, implying a route that it is possible to ride mountain bikes on, as in the expression 'rail trail', meaning an old railway line that's now become a route for cyclists on mountain bikes. Or something even gentler, such as wine trail or a heritage trail. So, if you are walking along a trail in New Zealand there's a chance that you might soon be startled by some executive type in orange Lycra. But if you are on a track you probably won't see any cyclists. The distinction isn't hard and fast, though: the Kauaeranga Kauri Trail (Chapter Thirteen) has hundreds of steps!

Blog Post with More Information

a-maverick.com/blog/new-zealand-travel-tips

TOUR 1: The Tail of the Fish

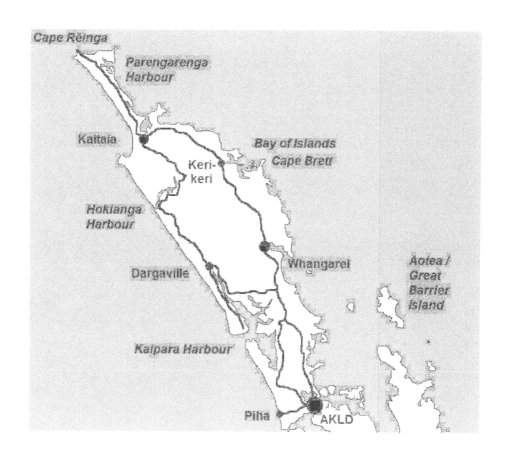

CHAPTER TWO

Spirits Bay and Sand Duning

SPIRITS BAY is in the far north of New Zealand, known to Māori as the 'tail of the fish', with subtropical white sandy beaches and fabulous sunrises and sunsets.

This beautiful area also serves as the starting point for the Te Paki Coastal Track, a walk of three to four days.

About halfway along the track you come to Cape Rēinga, also known as Te Rerenga Wairua, which is where the Pacific Ocean and Tasman Sea meet.

More significantly, Cape Rēinga is a sacred place. In Māori mythology it is considered to be the place where the spirits of the dead go to be cleansed and then leap off and enter the underworld to return to their eternal home of Hawaiki, also called Hawaiki-a-Nui, or Great Hawaiki. Interestingly enough, this heaven is also the Māori equivalent of the Garden of Eden: the place from which the ancestors of the Māori were said to have come to live in New Zealand, in a sense, as exiles.

Hawaiki is the local version of a suite of similar-sounding names that crop up all over tropical Polynesia such as Savai'i in Samoa and, of course, Hawai'i. To what extent these versions of the same name reflect actual migration history and kinship among

15

the islands, however, as opposed to shared Edenic myths, is debated still.

Te Rerenga Wairua means 'the place where the spirits fly' and Rēinga also means both the underworld and the leaping place of spirits.

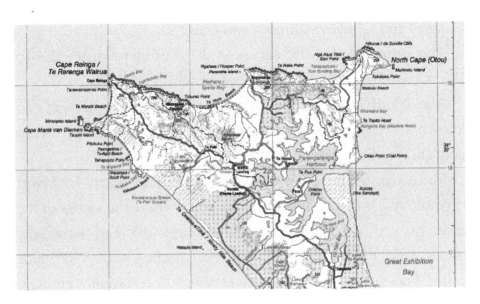

*The very northernmost tip of the North Island of New Zealand. Map data by LINZ via NZ Topo Map (**topomap.co.nz**), 2020.*

Spirits Bay is known in Māori as Piwhane or alternatively as Kapowairua, which means 'catch the spirits'. We stayed first at Kapowairua Spirits Bay Campsite, and from there walked eighteen kilometres along the coastal track to Tapotupotu Bay, close to Cape Rēinga.

Here are a couple of useful DOC web resources by the way. If you are reading this in print, just search for them on the DOC website:

Historic Cape Reinga, and, *Te Paki Coastal Track.*

The next place we camped was near Te Werahi Beach, about seven kilometres on. past the Cape and facing west (I can't over-emphasise the usefulness of camping apps to find these campsites!)

Then we walked on another ten kilometres to Te Paki Stream where we came out onto the immense sand dunes which people often boogie board on.

The Cape Rēinga Lighthouse

Crossing one of the several streams on the way

Other classic areas in this northern tip of the North Island are Parengarenga Harbour, famed for its clear water and white sands fronting onto Great Exhibition Bay on the east coast, and Ninety Mile Beach on the west coast, which isn't really ninety miles long but pretty long all the same!

The area around Cape Rēinga and Spirits Bay, and between Ninety Mile Beach and Great Exhibition Bay, is known more generally as the Aupori Peninsula.

In the next chapter, I'm going to be talking about the wider northern region of which the Aupori Peninsula is just the first, northernmost taste!

Blog post with more images:

a-maverick.com/blog/spirits-bay-and-sand-duning

CHAPTER THREE

The 'Winterless' North

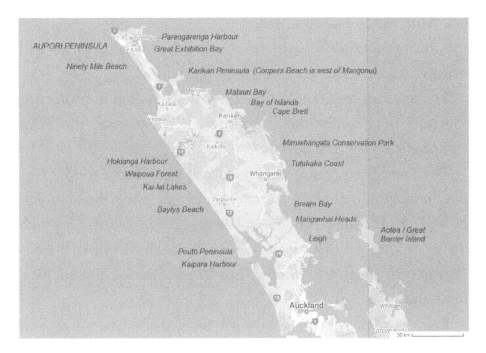

The 'Winterless' North. *Place names over water added for this book.*
Map data ©2029 Google

SOUTH of the long, thin Aupori peninsula is the main bulk of the part of New Zealand known as Te Tai Tokerau ('the north coast') or Northland, a region long dubbed the 'winterless north' by local tourism operators. This is almost true, even if it isn't literally true.

19

Northland used to be covered in kauri, a tree of great significance to Māori and esteemed as particularly valuable to loggers, partly because the oldest ones are huge and partly because the wood is rot-proof and easy to work as well, with a beautiful, honey-like appearance.

Kauri also produce hard resin called kauri gum, which had many decorative and industrial uses at one time.

The marine playground of the Bay of Islands and its protective southern breakwater, the Cape Brett peninsula, are the main attractions on the east coast.

The Cape Brett peninsula is of special significance to Māori as the branching-off place of the seven ancestral ocean-going canoes (double-hulled and more like catamaran yachts) on which the ancestors of the Māori were said to have arrived from Hawaiki, or in material terms, Eastern Polynesia, roughly one thousand years ago.

In the traditional story, the vessels arrived at the peninsula and then split up to settle different parts of New Zealand.

The Waipoua Forest, and the Bay of Islands and nearby Cape Brett, are just two places worth visiting in Northland. There's plenty more to this slow-paced region, which, in spite of its natural beauty and proximity to Auckland, still provides a range of fairly uncrowded and uncommercial experiences. Some other parts of New Zealand, such as Queenstown, are starting to become quite busy with international tourists. That isn't true of Northland – yet.

The Tallest Giant: Tāne Mahuta and the Waipoua Forest

Waipoua Forest is home to Tāne Mahuta, the tallest kauri tree in the world. Named after the god of the forest, Tāne Mahuta is over fifty metres tall and just under four and a half metres in diameter. Thought to be about two thousand years old, this immense tree is one of several impressive sights in the forest. These also include the second tallest kauri, Te Matua Ngahere, which means 'the father of the forest'.

Waipoua Forest makes up the largest remaining tract of native bush in the area together with the adjoining forests of Mataraua and Waima. At only 65 km from Dargaville, it can be easily reached by car via State Highway 12, which runs through the forest.

I once took Niels Lutyens, a friend and fellow voyager who I introduce in my first book *A Maverick Traveller,* to see the majestic kauri here. Looking up at the huge trees, you could see how Tāne Mahuta and Te Matua Ngahere got their names.

These days, one thing I've noticed is the growing prevalence of dead and dying kauri: the consequence of kauri dieback disease, a spreading malady that was probably imported into the country some decades ago. And evidence of belated official attempts to deal with the problem.

See the freely available article by Bob Harvey, 'Death of the gods: the woeful response to Kauri dieback disease', *Metro* magazine (Auckland), 20 February 2019.

Tāne Mahuta

The Bay of Islands and Cape Brett

Bay of Islands, Cape Brett peninsula, and environs. Names of Cape Brett, Deep Water Cove and Rākaumangamanga added for this book. Map data ©2018 Google.

One of the most famous places in New Zealand is the Bay of Islands. As its name suggests, this gorgeous bay on the east coast of Northland is full of islands. It is shielded from cold southern winds, any that make it this far north, by Cape Brett.

The Bay of Islands was the seat of New Zealand's very first capital at Russell; and is the site of the Treaty House, where the founding Treaty of Waitangi was signed on the 6th of February, 1840, between Queen Victoria's representatives and a number of Māori rangatira, or chieftains.

23

Nowadays, the Bay is a hugely scenic, classic holiday destination with lots of interesting islands as the name suggests; and also plenty of evidence of its history, including an old stone store dating back to the 1830s in the nearby town of Kerikeri.

I stopped in first at the Bland Bay Motor Camp near Whangaruru, which is toward the bottom right of the map just above. This area, south of the Cape Brett peninsula, is a refuge from the busier and more commercialised Bay of Islands proper.

The Bland Bay Motor Camp is run by the Ngāti Wai iwi, or tribal group. I went for beautiful walks around Bland Bay and nearby Puriri Bay.

I stayed there for three days just relaxing, but then I thought that I had to take up the challenge of tramping the length of the Cape Brett peninsula toward its jagged, seven-peaked tip known as Rākaumangamanga.

The Māori word rākau means tree or stick, while manga means branch. Doubling up the word manga adds emphasis. In this way, Rākaumangamanga means 'the branching-off place of the canoes'. The seven peaks of Rākaumangamanga also represent the original colonising fleet.

However many vessels there were in actuality and whether they all came at once or in stages, the legend is thought to be founded in fact: that Rākaumangamanga probably was an important rendezvous point in the old days when Polynesians first came to New Zealand, as it juts far out to sea and is hard to miss or mistake for any other place on the coast when you are sailing south-westwards toward New Zealand from tropical Polynesia.

On the subject of tramping the Cape Brett peninsula – where the whole human history of New Zealand is thus said to have begun – the first thing to mention is that the track takes about eight hours from start to finish.

In several places it gets gnarly and exposed, with big drop-offs to either side, though the views are terrific.

There are several carparks at the beginning. A lot of cars get robbed, though you can pay NZ $8, currently, for more secure parking. The first section runs along Māori communal land, and then you get into conservation areas. There is a stream and a water tank half along the track, but carrying water is recommended. I would recommend carrying water purification pills as well.

You can make side-trips from the main track to the old Whangamumu Bay whaling station and other areas of interest. Whangamumu Bay is well worth it, a white sand beach sheltered by two peninsulas that act as natural breakwaters.

The remarkable Whangamumu Bay, guarded between two natural breakwaters

Further along, you get to Deep Water Cove on the western side, which has terrific views of the Bay of Islands. This also be enjoyed from a strategically-located toilet, though only with the door open of course.

For those who don't want parking hassles or too long a walk, it's possible to take a water taxi from various Bay of Islands localities such as Russell, Paihia and Oke Bay to Deep Water Cove or Cape Brett. One advantage of taking the water taxi all the way to or from Cape Brett is that if sea conditions allow, the taxi may go through the famous 'Hole in the Rock' at Motukōkako (Piercy Island) just off Cape Brett.

The 'hole in the rock' through Motukōkako (Piercy Island), with Otuwhanga Island and Cape Brett behind. By Matt Lemmon on Wikimedia Commons, CC-BY-SA 2.0, 12 January 2008.

The author by the Cape Brett Lighthouse and Otuwhanga Island, Motukōkako (Piercy Island) and Tiheru Island. Thrilled to be there!

Near the Cape Brett Lighthouse is the so-called Cape Brett Hut, overlooked by the massive looming presence of Otuwhanga Island. Rather flash as huts go, it used to be the lighthouse keeper's house, of course.

It's necessary to book the hut in advance if you want to stay there. It has a combination lock, and you get the combination on booking.

I saw a stoat running along the track. Fingers of land like the Cape Brett peninsula are obvious candidates for being fenced off and made predator-free. It's a sign of DOC funding stress that they aren't.

There is also a fee for walking across the Māori land, which goes toward the maintenance of the track on that section.

The fee can also be avoided by taking the water taxi both ways, though this means missing out on a portion of the track.

Whangārei and the rest of Northland

If you travel up the east coast from Auckland, you get to Leigh Marine Reserve, which is very much worth a visit with its reef and glass-bottom boat tours.

Check out the local website, **leighbythesea.co.nz**.

North of Leigh there's some really scenic coast with offshore islands, past Mangawhai Heads and up Bream Bay.

The biggest city in Northland is Whangārei, with a population of about 55,000 in the city and 80,000 in its surrounding area. There are some really nice tracks just in and around the city, such as climbing Mount Parihaka close to town and Mount Manaia closer to the harbour heads, the Otaika Valley Walk and the Abbey Caves and the Whangārei Falls. Of all New Zealand's cities Whangārei seems to be the one that's actually built on scenic attractions and outdoor opportunities the most.

Whangārei is also the gateway to the Tutukaka Coast, which National Geographic Travel lately rated as one of the top three coastal destinations in the world.

From the Tutukaka Coast you can see the Poor Knights Islands, which are rated as one of the world's top diving spots as well.

Further north towards the Bay of Islands, there is the Mimiwhangata Coastal Park.

Basically, the entire coast of Northland is one of mountains and stunning beaches.

Near the Bay of Islands, the town of Kawakawa has toilets designed by the Austrian hippie architect Friedensreich Hundertwasser and also has a railway line going up its main street, the last town in New Zealand to have that sort of olden-days arrangement. The railway is operated today by the Bay of Islands Vintage Railway Trust.

Street entrance to the Hundertwasser-Toilets at Kawakawa, public domain image by Reinhard Dietrich, February 2012 via Wikimedia Commons

North of the Bay of Islands there's Matauri Bay and Coopers Beach, more classic holiday destinations. Coopers Beach is in Doubtless Bay, sheltered by the Karikari Peninsula, which has several beaches of its own.

West of Coopers Beach, Kaitaia is the northernmost sizeable town in New Zealand.

Coming down the wilder, less developed west coast, you come to the very historic Hokianga Harbour just north of the location of Tāne Mahuta, which has many attractions and lookouts of its own including the Waimamaku Coastal Track.

Near Kaikohe, in the centre of Northland, there's Ngāwhā Springs.

Further down the west coast are the beautiful Kai Iwi Lakes. White sand and clear water, basically rainwater.

At Matakohe, near Dargaville, there is an amazing museum dedicated to the kauri logging and gum digging that used to be common in the area. Dargaville itself is rated as New Zealand's 'kūmara capital', the centre of sweet potato cultivation. From Dargaville you can head due west a short distance to Baylys Beach. South of Dargaville, at the tip of the Pouto Peninsula which shields the northern part of the vast Kaipara Harbour, it's possible to go sand duning again, just as it is near Spirits Bay.

For people who like things hippyish, Kaiwaka, closer to Auckland, has the Eutopia Café. This has lately been redecorated and is now really attractive inside.

Blog posts with more images:

a-maverick.com/blog/the-winterless-north

a-maverick.com/blog/cape-brett-hiking-to-the-birthplace-of-aotearoa

Some additional online resources

WhangareiNZ.com (good visitor website for Whangārei, with local walks)

WhangareiNZ.com Te Whara / Bream Head Track (This looks amazing! And yet it's right next to Whangārei.)

WhangareiNZ.com, Visitor Information

DOC: *Te Matua Ngahere Walk*

DOC: *Waipoua Forest*

DOC: *Waimamaku Coastal Track*

DOC: *Mimiwhangata Coastal Park*

NorthlandNZ.com (good overall visitor website)

nzpocketguide.com, *12 Whangarei walks you can't miss*

Whangārei District Council Walks and Trails Guide

newzealand.com, Whangārei Heads

Heritage New Zealand, Path to Nationhood (historical tour apps)

Bay of Islands Vintage Railway Trust

THE NEGLECTED NORTH ISLAND

CHAPTER FOUR

'Tossed by the Wind': The rare and remarkable creatures of Tiritiri Matangi Island

TIRITIRI Matangi is a small island in the Hauraki Gulf, four kilometres off the coast north of Auckland, where I went to serve as a New Zealand Department of Conservation (DOC) volunteer.

Tiritiri Matangi means 'tossed by the wind', a phrase in which the word for wind is matangi. Hauraki, a name I'll be referring to in other chapters as well, looks quite different but also refers to the wind. Hauraki means 'north wind' using another word for wind, hau.

Tiritiri Matangi was farmed for many years, but in 1971 it was given to the government to become a recreation reserve and is now a nature reserve where the public can stay.

The development of the reserve has been a huge success for conservation and there are now well-established populations of many sorts of rare birds and other animals, as well as plants.

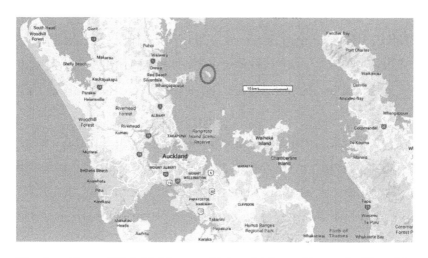

The location of Tiritiri Matangi Island (ringed by red ellipse) in Auckland's Hauraki Gulf. Map data ©2019 Google.

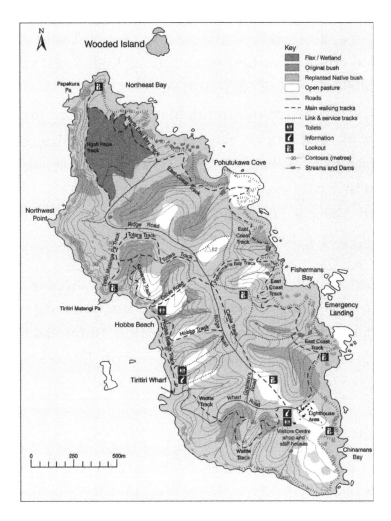

Map of Tiritiri Matangi Island. (DOC, 2017)

There is an older and larger island reserve further out in the Hauraki Gulf, called Hauturu or Little Barrier Island. But Hauturu / Little Barrier has long been closed to the general public. The champions of the new reserve at Tiritiri Matangi wanted to create something more accessible, an open sanctuary that would create community buy-in.

The precedent set by Tiritiri Matangi has since inspired a number of other open sanctuaries, including Maungatautari and Zealandia in Wellington, both of which I am going to talk about in later chapters of this book.

Tiritiri Matangi now gets 30,000 visitors a year, a number bulked up by regular school tours.

The most useful website for the island is the site of the Supporters of Tiritiri Matangi, on **tiritirimatangi.org.nz**. The Supporters' website includes historical information and instructions on how to book accommodation. For tickets to get there, go to **fullers.co.nz**.

My Visits

I spent a week on the island as a volunteer DOC warden in the summer of 2011–2012. (In New Zealand, Christmas and New Year are in the middle of summer.) And I'd been to the island before that.

I enjoyed helping out, that summer. But there's nothing like being a guest and being left to your own devices, which was my experience when I came back in later years.

They have about sixteen bunks for the public on Tiritiri Matangi and it gets very busy during the summer, which is great for fundraising and everything. On the other hand, I prefer the off-season.

The Tiritiri Matangi lighthouse is a tremendously historic piece of industrial heritage by New Zealand standards, designed in 1861 and first illuminated on New Year's Day, 1865. Made from cast-iron prefabricated panels, it must have been a very modern structure by the standards of its day.

The Tiritiri Matangi lighthouse and adjoining structures, including a signal tower built in 1912

Until 1947 it was painted red, appearing dark in old photographs, and there is some talk of painting it red once more.

The night hunters

It's worth going out on the tracks at night. That's how I've managed to spot kiwi, for instance.

*The Little Spotted Kiwi, historic engraving by J. G. Keulemans, from G. D. Rowley's **Ornithological Miscellany** via nzbirds.com and Wikimedia Commons. Public domain image.*

Kiwi are omnivores, feeding on anything that is small and nutritious. Unusually for a bird, they rely heavily on smell, sniffing out their food at ground level with nostrils at the tips of their long, probing beaks. They have powerful claws, which they use to demolish old tree stumps and rotting logs to get at the grubs inside.

There are five living species of kiwi, of much the same shape but of different sizes and colourations. The little spotted kiwi I saw is the smallest. The largest is the southern brown kiwi or tokoeka, which is divided further into two subspecies of slightly differing sizes.

I've seen a little blue penguin at night as well. This is the world's smallest species of penguin. It was high tide and the penguin was just sitting on the track, which was almost deserted at night. There are breeding boxes for the little blue penguins beside the track, so you can often see the penguins there too.

And tuatara: two of them.

The tuatara is a cat-eyed nocturnal reptile that looks like a lizard.—. but isn't!

Although the tuatara looks like a lizard, the resemblance is really only skin-deep, and there are lots of differences underneath. In fact, tuatara are the last survivors of a group of reptiles called rynchocephalia which evolved in the Triassic era, before the evolution of mammals and at about the same time as the very earliest dinosaurs.

The birds of the day

Many New Zealand songbirds feed on nectar. However, the habitat on Tiritiri Matangi isn't rich enough for nectar-feeding birds to thrive and produce large numbers of young without supplementation.

So, there are a lot of artificial nectar stations on the island. The artificial feeding stations dispense a mixture of water and raw sugar, which contains many micronutrients absent from the refined sugar and thus approximates the nectar found in flowers. Diluted honey might be closer to the real thing, but it would obviously be a lot more expensive. The raw sugar used on Tiritiri Matangi is donated by the local firm Chelsea Sugar, who have an informative webpage on the subject.

In terms of physical proportions, the takahē is a turkey to the pūkeko's hen. It also tends to live on more solid ground, as it would sink into any swamp.

Takahē were thought to be extinct for a long time, but a population was rediscovered in the late 1940s, west of Lake Te Anau in the South Island. They are slowly coming back from the brink and are now a fairly common sight in bird sanctuaries across New Zealand.

Today, Tiritiri Matangi is an important breeding centre for hihi and other endangered species.

I finally saw a pair of kōkako on the Wattle Track, but they were too deep in the bush for me to take a photo. Still, I heard their peculiar, low song. I was told that there were eighteen pairs but that they avoid the visitors. I had the same experience on the Kawerau Track.

Kōkako are called the 'squirrels' and sometimes even the 'monkeys' of the New Zealand forest: disdaining to fly (though they can) and preferring to clamber about instead. They are very agile climbers. All you normally see of a kōkako is a shadow, something moving across the tree canopy without taking to the air, concealed by the leaves and the limbs.

So, the kōkako were too elusive for me to see much of them or get any pictures.

Even more elusive are the fernbirds, tiny birds that are almost flightless (which is very unusual for small birds) and which scuttle about like mice. There were no mice in old-time New Zealand, so the fernbirds evolved to take their place.

The Proud Supporters

The volunteers from the Supporters of Tiritiri Matangi are very proud of their work, and one lady, a long-time volunteer, even told me that it was *her* island and we shouldn't trust the government with it, as they were the ones who had let the bird population dwindle until there was almost none left. They couldn't look after the birds, and they couldn't look after the island. She was very territorial – but with a beautiful, natural place like Tiritiri Matangi Island, I can almost see why.

Some final tips

Tripadvisor says that coming to Tiritiri Matangi is one of the top things to do in Auckland and has awarded the island its Certificate of Excellence. Well, that's really interesting.

They take your packs up to the bunkhouse by trailer when you arrive by ferry, and when the ferry returns, they will take your pack down. And on the ferry, you can buy food such as sandwiches and muffins. But beware, the store on Tiritiri Matangi does not sell any food whatsoever. Along with souvenirs, they sell drinks and that's it. They have a policy of not selling food.

Instead, the emphasis is on providing an educational area for children, with lots of seating. School parties bring their own lunches.

The Supporters of Tiritiri Matangi have plans for a new field centre. This field centre will have eleven two-bed units for visitors and two two-bedroom family units, but still with shared cooking. There will be three self-contained units for staff. The complex will be on Wharf Road.

Blog posts with more images:

a-maverick.com/blog/tossed-by-the-wind-the-rare-and-remarkable-creatures-of-tiritiri-matangi-part-one

a-maverick.com/blog/tossed-wind-tiritiri-matangi-part-two

CHAPTER FIVE

Aotea, or Great Barrier Island (not the Great Barrier Reef)

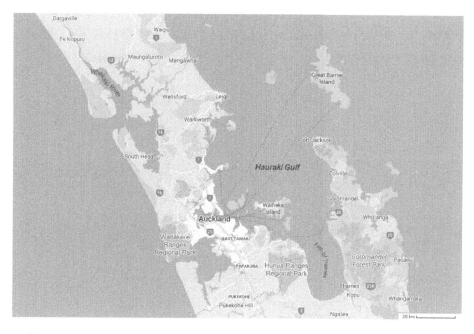

The Hauraki Gulf and its Islands. *Name of the Hauraki Gulf added for this book. Map Data ©2020 Google.*

LARGEST of Auckland's Hauraki Gulf Islands is Great Barrier Island, also known as Aotea, the island of the white cloud or the shining sky. When I get tele-marketing calls selling holidays on Australia's Great Barrier Reef, I tell them, 'We have our own Great Barrier Island.' I don't tell them it's not so big!

Nor is it as polluted. Great Barrier Island comes in near the top of coastal destinations rated by *National Geographic* in 2010:

"Only 55 miles of ocean separate Great Barrier Island from cosmopolitan Auckland, but given how little the two places have in common, the distance seems much greater. With less than 1,000 permanent residents, more than half of its land area administered by New Zealand's Department of Conservation, and fewer introduced species than elsewhere in the country, the island is in good shape ecologically and will likely remain so for a while."[1]

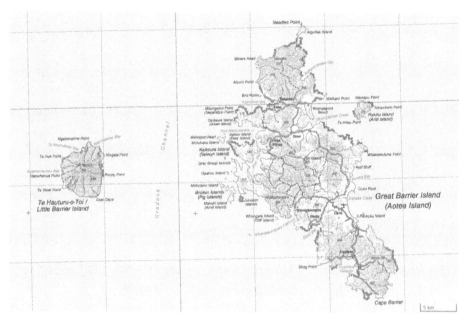

Little and Great Barrier Islands. Map data by LINZ via <u>NZ Topo Map</u>, *2020.*

Located 90 km (55 miles) north-east of Auckland on the edge of the Hauraki Gulf Marine Park, New Zealand's 'National Park of the Sea', the island can be reached by a 4-hour ferry ride, or a scenic half-hour flight from Auckland International Airport.

There is a useful tourism website on **greatbarrierisland.nz** which includes an app that can be downloaded from **app.greatbarrierisland.nz**. Another useful tourism website, **greatbarrier.co.nz**, includes information on how to get to Aotea / Great Barrier Island.

Over the years, I've loved going over to the island and tramping the 621-metre high Mount Hobson, also known by its Māori name of Hirakimata, as well as visiting other parts of the island.

There are no possums, stoats or ferrets on the island, which means that despite the few remaining rats the forest is largely untouched. The island is beautiful, with jagged green mountains like those seen on Polynesian islands in the tropics and huge nīkau palms – the only palm endemic to New Zealand (in two species) and the southernmost palm in the world, growing to 44 degrees south. Furthermore, Great Barrier or Aotea Island is so far off the beaten track that it doesn't really get a lot of city slickers and is the perfect place to get away for a break.

Whale Sighting off Great Barrier Island

Views and Pools

Several of the most popular destinations on the island are on a scenic pathway known as the Aotea Track. These include the peak of Hirakimata, and Windy Canyon, a *Lord of the Rings* filming site, I walked a part of the Aotea Track in January 2015 with my friend Rose and her partner, Daniel. We hiked along it to the top of Hirakimata, where there are amazing 360-degree views of the island. There are also free hot pools located on a section of the track that leads from the Whangaparapara Road to Hirakimata: the Kaitoke hot pools.

Making our way to Hirakimata

It's worth staying at Mount Heale Hut, which is a back-country hut with all kitchen implements, pots, pans, and even a dish brush supplied.—.and a view to die for!

Dark Skies

Aotea/Great Barrier Island is now a Dark Sky Sanctuary. There are twelve International Dark-Sky Association Dark Sky Reserves including one at Lake Tekapo in New Zealand, but only three Dark Sky Sanctuaries, astronomical viewing sites which are even more pristine.

The three Dark Sky Sanctuaries are at Cosmic Campground in New Mexico, at the Elqui Valley in northern Chile, and now at Great Barrier Island as well.

The locals hope that Dark Sky Sanctuary status will increase winter tourism as well, since in winter the nights are longer. At that time of year, it's also possible to see the core of the Milky Way, which lies in the constellations of Scorpio and Sagittarius; whereby the Milky Way comes to look like a poached egg seen side-on rather than just a band of stars.

The Milky Way panorama. European Southern Observatory (ESO). CC-BY-SA 4.0 (original webpage *eso.org/public/images/eso0932a/*)

You can get apps for viewing the dark sky such as Star Chart, recommended by the government tourist organisation, 100% Pure New Zealand: "New Zealand is famous for Dark Sky Reserves. Simply point your device to the night sky and virtual stars and planets will appear through the app. See exactly what is in the sky and learn fun facts about the constellations.

Blog post with more images:

a-maverick.com/blog/aucklands-great-barrier-island-not-the-great-barrier-reef

Reference Note

1 Great Barrier Island Tourism, 'National Geographic gives Great Barrier Island the Thumbs Up', 9 February 2015; *National Geographic,* 'Coastal Destinations Rated: Top Rated', 20 October 2010.

CHAPTER SIX

Auckland's Icon: Rangitoto

RANGITOTO Island is a short ferry ride from downtown Auckland city. This beautiful, rocky, island is New Zealand's youngest volcano, emerging from the sea only 600 years ago. Rangitoto has since become a safe haven for wildlife, with a dedicated effort at pest eradication made by DOC before they finally declared the island to be pest-free in 2011. In this natural paradise, there are a range of walks you can do either around the island or to the 260 metre (850 feet) high summit where there are great views of Auckland harbour and the Hauraki Gulf.

Rangitoto – a volcanic desert island in the middle of a city harbour.
(Map Data ©2020 Google)

You can see Rangitoto Island from many places in Auckland. The island is almost perfectly round and symmetrical. This map gives you a better idea of just how much it dominates the eastern beaches.

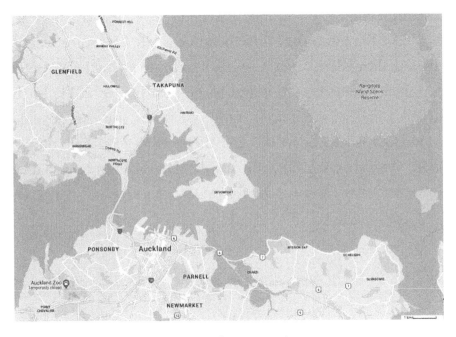

Map data ©2020 Google

Rangitoto Island is entirely covered in dark green jungle rising out of rocky black basalt, like a scene from tropical Polynesia.

As with all the islands near Auckland, you can get to Rangitoto from the city's rather San Francisco-like downtown ferry building. There is a tourism website, **rangitoto.co.nz**, which includes information on how to book transport to and from the island. The Department of Conservation also has a web resource called *Rangitoto Island*.

Auckland Ferry Terminal as seen from the harbour. *Photo by Alexander Klink, 17 March 2006, CC-BY-3.0 via Wikimedia Commons.*

There's a rich set of ferry routes in Auckland Harbour, shown on Google Maps.

Auckland Harbour Ferries. *Destinations added for this book where not shown already. Map data ©2020 Google.*

However, it's worth noting that not all the ferry routes appear on the Auckland Transport website (**at.govt.nz**), only the ones relevant to suburban commuters. Auckland ferry services are run by Fullers and SeaLink: it pays to check their websites directly for ferries that run further afield and to resort islands, nature reserves and Aotea/Great Barrier Island and the Coromandel Peninsula.

It was probably upon Rangitoto that John Logan Campbell, the city's principal nineteenth-century founder, was gazing when, as recorded by the historian Russell Stone in *The Father and His Gift,* Campbell wrote to his wife Emma that "Today is one of

Auckland's ravishing days of exquisite beauty, enough to make a man foreswear [sic] heaven & worship the beauty of the lower earth."

I also took some pictures of the island on a recent ramble through the eastern suburbs.

The only thing spoiling the symmetry is the fact that another island, Motutapu ('Sacred Island'), is just behind Rangitoto and can generally be seen peeping around its right flank.

Rangitoto is only about six hundred years old! The island erupted from the harbour, from scratch, in the days when Māori were as yet Auckland's only occupants. Amazingly, human and dog footprints filled in by ash from the erupting Rangitoto have been found preserved on Motutapu.

Rangitoto erupted only once, and then fell silent. This is typical of Auckland's volcanoes. Early colonists were fooled into supposing that Auckland's volcanism was as extinct as the volcanoes on which Edinburgh is built.

In reality, there will be a next volcano in Auckland. It's just that nobody knows where and nobody knows when.

It's incredible to think that island is a huge, unspoilt volcanic island right in the middle of Auckland Harbour!

First stop is the jetty and the welcome signs.

You can get a vehicle to the summit, a sort of rover vehicle with trailers, or you can hike it if you want. When you get to the top, there's a huge crater.

The island used to have a penal colony on it, and there are still a few old structures from that time.

The overwhelming impression is barren rocky basalt, on which vegetation somehow manages to grow. If you could image the moon with trees on it, that's pretty much what Rangitoto is like. It looks greener side-on than up close, because when you are there you can see the rocks between the trees. It gets quite hot in the full sun.

I hiked along the coastal track to a place called Boulder Bay and had a swim.

Boulder Bay is on the north-eastern side of Rangitoto Island. That means that, if Rangitoto Island is like the moon with trees, Boulder Bay is on the far side of the moon.

There is no sign of the city of 1.6 million people on this side of Rangitoto Island. You might as well be in the most deserted part of the South Pacific.

Sadly, you can't have everything and what Rangitoto doesn't have is anything resembling a decent beach anywhere!

In spite of all that, lots of people came to get away from it all in the past, and to erect small holiday homes, or baches. Bach is a Kiwi word which comes from 'bachelor' and implies a small place big enough for a single man but not big enough for a family to live respectably. The term probably originated in the early days of mining and logging, but later on it came to mean a holiday home into which the whole family would be squeezed for a few weeks.

People eventually decided that the baches were part of the island's heritage. The baches even started getting plaques and an honourable mention from UNESCO!

There's a World War II-era lookout with old black and white photographs of the soldiers assigned to that boring-but-safe job, and also what we call a 'trig station', used by surveyors in the region to check their exact location by measuring the angle to two or more trig stations from where they were.

I wonder if the old soldiers ever thought they'd have this much company.

Looking in the other direction, we can see Motutapu Island, which is agricultural: completely different to Rangitoto. And Waiheke behind it, along with other islands and mountain ranges.

Oh yes, one last thing. The top of Rangitoto Island was where the Auckland Tramping Club was founded, initially on terms that excluded women. No girls allowed in this boys' treehouse. Quite comical today but it certainly put the bachelor into bach, I guess!

Blog post with more images:

a-maverick.com/blog/aucklands-icon-rangitoto-island-the-harbour-volcano

CHAPTER SEVEN

An Undeveloped Gem: Auckland's Rotoroa Island

L AST summer, my father and I decided to visit Rotoroa Island. It's a small, beautiful island in the Hauraki Gulf east of downtown Auckland.

Ferries regularly depart for the island from downtown Auckland: which always looks grey and dull compared to the fabulous gulf, and other downtowns as well.

The flag on the back of the boat brings out the contrast.

We sailed past the lovely, unspoilt volcanic cone of Rangitoto Island, and arrived at Rotoroa Island.

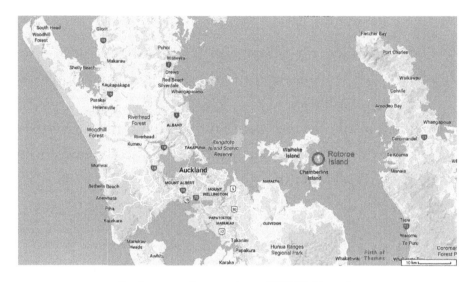

Background map data ©2019 Google

Rotoroa Island has lots of walking tracks and, unlike Rangitoto, nice beaches too. I walked all around the island apart from the North Tower Loop Track, which was closed.

You can see the tracks and beaches in a photo of a signboard on the island, which follows on the next page.

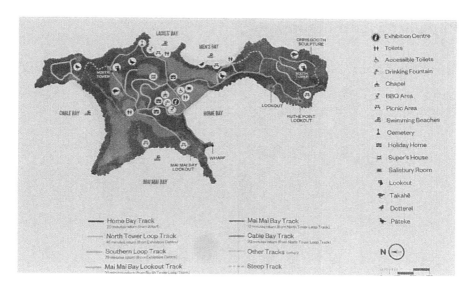

Rotoroa Island, on a local information panel

Rotoroa is just as charming as many more touristy parts of the Gulf and *isn't* overdeveloped! Ironically, its use as a treatment centre spared it from the ravages of ticky-tacky development.

Though it isn't highly developed, Rotoroa does have some accommodation: it's not just for day trippers. It's really a beautiful spot to get away from it all.

> You can get all the information you need about the island, including travel and accommodation details, from **rotoroa.org.nz**.

Blog post with more images:

a-maverick.com/blog/an-undeveloped-gem-aucklands-rotoroa-island

CHAPTER EIGHT

Sunrise on a City Beach

N EW ZEALAND is one of the first places to see the new day, being so far east. And there are lots of good places to see it from, even just in Auckland.

Here's a map showing the area I visited on this trip, inside the red box.

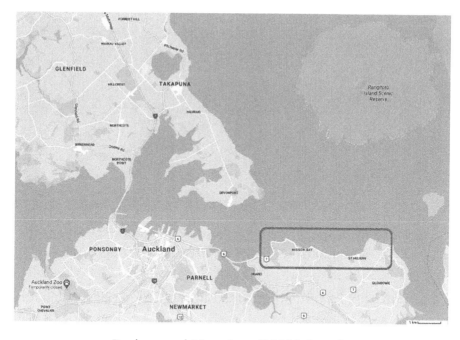

Background Map data ©2020 Google.

Kohimarama Beach is the long beach, and Ōkahu Bay is the westward facing bay at the far left where highway number 7 is indicated.

These are great spots for seeing the sunrise, because they look out over water to the north and to the east. And because you can see the great, green volcano of Rangitoto Island, and the other islands of the city's eastern approaches, which are known as the Hauraki Gulf.

Auckland from Space. Satellite photography is from NASA Earth Observatory Image Auckland_17_2002239.

I got up at 5:30 a.m. and arrived in the suburb of St Heliers at the eastern end of Kohimarama Beach at six. I was amazed at the number of joggers out and that the cafes were already open, with first responders having takeaway coffee on the park benches.

There was a great opportunity to read the *New Zealand Herald* and have a cappuccino after I'd done my hike.

The sun began to peep up by the time I got to Mission Bay at the western end of Kohimarama Beach.

Mission Bay includes a memorial to the much-loved Prime Minister who guided New Zealand out of the Great Depression of the 1930s, Michael Joseph Savage.

Savage died during World War II and was interred under the huge memorial.

It's on a hill, and I had to climb up to get to it.

A park surrounds the monument, all on top of the hill. It's almost worth being dead for, to be commemorated like that!

You can get a view of the city centre and the Auckland Harbour Bridge.

This area, known as Bastion Point, or as Kohimarama or Takaparawhā in Māori, is also the site of a famous Māori land dispute and protest action that took place in 1978.

And finally, Ōkahu Bay.

I was amazed. All along, Rangitoto was in the background and the other Hauraki Gulf Islands. "All save the face of man is divine" is another remark that the early founder John Logan Campbell made about Auckland and its harbour, reported by Stone. The city's natural setting was gorgeous but, still,

"I would not allow my two girls to remain & run the risk of being 'colonial' . . ."

Too late for me, I guess!

Blog post with more images:

a-maverick.com/blog/best-places-see-sunrise-auckland-new-zealand-part-1-citys-eastern-beaches

CHAPTER NINE

Two Inner-City Volcanoes

YOU can also see the sunrise from two of Auckland's pretty green volcanoes, Ōwairaka and Mount Eden.

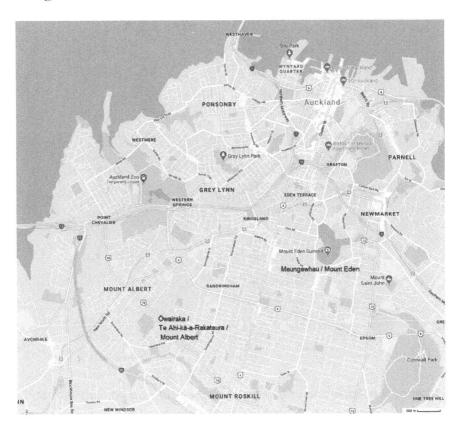

Auckland's inner suburbs, with Ōwairaka and Mount Eden identified (full official names). Background Map data ©2020 Google.

Auckland's an unusual city, because it's built on a field of extinct volcanoes, as per this famous map from 1859. The individual volcanoes are extinct, but there's always a risk a new one might pop up.

Map of the Auckland volcanic field by Ferdinand von Hochstetter, first published in 1859, from an 1865 reprint. Public domain image via Wikimedia Commons. Mount Eden, officially Maungawhau / Mount Eden, is 196 metres or 643 feet above sea level at the top. Ōwairaka, officially Ōwairaka / Te Ahi-kā-a-Rakataura / Mount Albert, is 135 metres or 443 feet.

So, the volcanoes are fairly small.

All the same, you can get amazing views. I would say that Mount Eden is the best place to get an overall view of Auckland as the sun comes up, because it's fairly close to the downtown with its tall buildings and Sky Tower.

You can watch the lights of the city centre, north of Mount Eden, slowly fade as the sun comes up over the suburbs to the east.

Mount Eden has a huge crater at the top. It's not as big as the crater on Rangitoto Island, but much more accessible. You can drive to the top, and there are bronze markers that point out where various local landmarks and distant cities are.

Here's a daytime photo of the same scene, showing a bit more of the crater.

Mount Eden's crater is called Te Ipo o Matāho, which means the mixing bowl of Matāho, a legendary hero. As the legend has it, the other volcanoes of Auckland were formed when Matāho's wife left him and took his clothes, so the fire-goddess Mahuika sent earth-fires to keep him warm.

The other thing that's really distinctive about Mount Eden is its pre-European terraces, which make it look a little bit like a Mayan stepped pyramid.

Terraces on Maungawhau / Mount Eden. Photo by 'Avenue', 2006, CC-BY-SA 3.0 and other licences via Wikimedia Commons.

Some of the other volcanoes of Auckland have terraces as well. World Heritage status has been applied for and it's being worked through.

Mount Eden is the most usual name of one of the peaks I went up. That name honours George Eden, the first Earl of Auckland (UK); its Māori name, Maungawhau, means 'mountain of the whau tree' (*Entelea arborescens*).

The other peak is known as Mount Albert, after Prince Albert; but most commonly these days by the name Ōwairaka. This name honours Wairaka, the daughter of a chief who sailed to New Zealand from Hawaiki, the legendary ancestral home of the Māori and returning-place of departed spirits.

And so that is the origin of Ōwairaka. The third official name for that volcano, Te Ahi-kā-a-Rakataura, means the home fires of Rakataura. This refers to a tohunga (shaman) who was named Rakataura.

When I went up Ōwairaka, there was a protest camp there, organised by a group called Honour the Maunga, whose protest signs included a picture of another volcano lately reduced to its bald state of a hundred years ago.

Such was the protest camp. In the next chapter, I'll be talking about how Covid lockdown forced me to rediscover even more of my immediate neighbourhood!

Blog post with more images:

a-maverick.com/blog/15-best-places-to-see-the-sunrise-in-auckland-two-inner-city-volcanoes

CHAPTER TEN

What can you find within Five Kilometres of your House?

THIS chapter is about exploring and discovering local places within five kilometres of the Auckland suburb of Point Chevalier. Which is as far afield as I was allowed to roam even for exercise, along with five million other New Zealanders, during the Coronavirus lockdown.

On the next page, I show the outer limit of my former five-kilometre exercise bubble, more or less, wrapped around an even more local area that I'm going to talk about in detail.

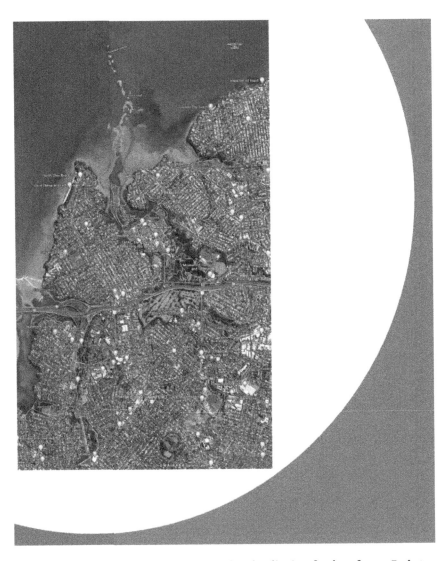

The shift from white to red marks the limit of 5 km from Point Chevalier, approximately. Aerial Imagery ©2020 CNES/Airbus, Maxar Technologies, Planet.com, Waikato District Council [sic], Map data ©2020 Google.

Where to go?

As it became clear that movement was going to be restricted. I started thinking about local travel destinations. Where could I go to get out of the house?

I took out the old bike I'd bought once upon a time from KMart (like Wal-Mart) and used WD-40 to oil it up. The wheels and the handlebars still work and so do the brakes, luckily. But the seat does not sit still.

But where could you possibly go within five kilometres?

Well, actually, lots of places as it turned out. Microscopic examination of even my local suburb in Auckland turned up a lot of surprises.

What did I discover?

A waterfall on Oakley Creek, above the underground motorway.

Ducks feeding. Native trees being planted. And a park that was now part of a marine reserve, next to the great motorway junction.

There were marine birds rarely seen in the city, such as stilts and the Variable Oystercatcher, found only in New Zealand. This was probably because the area is now part of the Motu Manawa-Pollen Island Marine Reserve.

And another park, at a place called Western Springs where the city used to get its water, where the gulls and ducks had taken over the benches and the seats.

I did a coastal walk around the Meola Estuary, with its reef.

I saw swans that I'd never seen before near Garnet Road; and discovered a path that followed the estuary from Meola Rd to Lemington Rd.

From Point Chevalier Beach to Coxs Bay via the Meola Creek. Detail *from aerial imagery above. The name 'Lemington Rd' has been added for this book*

And Point Chevalier Beach. Point Chevalier used to be a well-known beach resort for Aucklanders, a sort of mini-Bondi, busy as anything. At least it was until we started taking our holidays and weekends further afield.

Unknown photographer. (n.d.) Point Chevalier Beach. Auckland War Memorial Museum neg. C6599.

Sunset at Pt Chevalier Beach, wow, real dreamy!

There's plenty now to rediscover. and as maybe other people will rediscover it as well.

I've been all around the world myself, and it's great to get back to the places that are just about in my backyard. Once we're allowed to go further afield again, I'll be having a look at all the places that could be connected up to make a network for biking. I think that would really be a worthwhile project.

There are many other places to visit in Auckland while only travelling a short distance locally, or a longer one from other suburbs.

Other places to visit in Auckland include the picturesque North Shore suburb and naval base of Devonport.

And the 27 Regional Parks of Auckland, which are real gems won for us by earlier generations of politicians and added to lately.

82

Kawau Island, where Governor George Grey once lived. The Crystal Mountain Museum and Theme Park. And Waiheke Island, the largest island in the inner Hauraki Gulf, which has a regional park itself.

Here's a good guide from the Auckland Council: **aucklandcouncil.govt.nz/parks-recreation/get-outdoors**. You can find a list of the regional parks with app-type directions on how to get to them on **aucklandcouncil.govt.nz/parks-recreation/Pages/search-index.aspx.**

Auckland's 27 Regional Parks in the form of red disks with yellow centres. Background map data ©2020 Google.

There are also masses of cycleways in Auckland these days, both on the streets and in the parklands, where they shade into mountain biking trails.

This is a far cry from the way things were 25 years ago, when cyclists generally took potluck on the road and were not allowed into nature reserves either.

Auckland Transport (**at.govt.nz**) describes some of its cycle routes, with videos, on **at.govt.nz/about-us/campaigns/at-cycleways**. Auckland Transport also has a zoomable cycle map viewer, though as with the commuter ferry routes this only covers urban and suburban cycling, and not the more adventurous trails in rural reserves and parklands.

In the next two chapters, I visit two more Auckland destinations: Te Atatū, the peninsula of the risen dawn, and the incredible wilds of Auckland's west coast.

Blog posts with more images:

a-maverick.com/blog/what-can-you-find-within-five-kilometres-of-your-house

a-maverick.com/blog/devonport-new-zealand

a-maverick.com/blog/the-27-regional-parks-of-auckland

a-maverick.com/blog/waiheke-in-the-sun

a-maverick.com/blog/crystal-mountain

The Northern End of the Te Atatū Peninsula. *Imagery ©2020 CNES/Airbus, Landsat/Copernicus, Maxar Technologies, Google, Planet.com, Waikato Regional Council. Map data ©2020 Google.*

CHAPTER ELEVEN

The Peninsula of the Dawn: Te Atatū and its living mudflats

THE TE ATATŪ PENINSULA'S another natural wonder in the wild western suburbs of Auckland, New Zealand's largest city.

It's located between two creeks that meander lazily down to the upper Waitematā Harbour, the harbour of sparkling waters, across mud flats and through mangroves, for Auckland is subtropical enough to have mangroves, and other plants of a green and leathery character that seem to owe nothing to the modern urban civilization – with all its lawns and flower-beds – that has so lately sprung up in this part of the world.

Te Atatū wetland

These savage everglades of Auckland's upper Waitematā are one of the city's most appealing features, for some. They're not conventionally pretty beaches, though there are some.

More usual is mud.

Mud with mangroves.

The landscape's full of fresh-water swamps and salt marshes with boardwalks over the top.

The two creeks that define the peninsula are the Whau River, to the east, and Henderson Creek to the west. Whau is a kind of tree. As for Henderson Creek, it is named after an early settler of means who bought most of the land in the area from the colonial government in the 1850s.

I suspect that it was a long time before Mr Henderson was able to recoup much from his investment, as the area, though close to Auckland city, remained wild and frontier-like until the 1950s, inhabited only by a small number of Māori and settlers. That was mainly because the creeks, flowing from north to south, acted as powerful barriers to the westward expansion of the growing city of Auckland.

That problem persisted until the Whau River and Henderson Creek were finally crossed by the Northwestern Motorway in 1960.

Atatū is a Māori word meaning 'dawn (ata) arisen (tū)': Te Atatū means 'the dawn arisen'. For here, too, is a great place to see the sunrise ('ata') in Auckland. The word ata also means reflection. the sun rises – and reflects – over the great coppery fetch of the Waitematā Harbour. It's all very appropriate.

Just as in the days of the past, the modern Aucklanders are keen boaties.

In fact, it's something of a cliche that Auckland is the 'city of sails'. And not just sailboats. Powerboats and water-skiing are also allowed in the lower parts of Henderson Creek.

A lot of effort's going into the restoration of the mudflats, at one time thought of as unglamorous, but now seen as hugely important nurseries of life in the sea and also for the native birds, as well as healthy outdoor recreation.

One of the things that's happened with Covid lockdowns is that I find it a big hassle to drive anywhere far afield, now, after having not done so for a couple of months. I think this tendency to enjoy myself locally might last.

It'll be interesting to see if Aucklanders start to appreciate their city and its many interesting hidden-away places more, as opposed to travelling to some faraway destination for the nature cure.

Blog post with more images:

a-maverick.com/blog/the-peninsula-of-the-dawn-te-atatu-and-its-living-mudflats

CHAPTER TWELVE

Auckland's Western Wilds

L OCATED just a 30-minute drive west from downtown Auckland, the Hillary Trail is one of Auckland's best-kept secrets. It's too well kept a secret, really, as many Aucklanders have yet to experience it. Like me, they may take a long time to find it. Some Aucklanders, however, like the fact that it is a semi-secret.

Named after New Zealand's most famous explorer, Sir Edmund Hillary, whom a friend of mine has kindly sketched for this book, the track takes you through the Waitākere Ranges Regional Park, along wild coastline, past countless waterfalls, and through ancient bush.

Looking to explore the full length of the trail, some friends and I had an itinerary of four days and three nights, leaving from the Auckland suburb of Titirangi and heading through the

Arataki Visitor Centre to tramp to the Karamatura Valley Campsite just west of the coastal settlement of Huia.

The Hillary Trail and its Environs. *(Based on NASA Earth Observatory jpeg image Auckland_17_2002239). NB this is no substitute for a proper trail map.*

Titirangi is well worth stopping in for a cup of coffee. On the edge of the city, this suburb is already well into the primordial bush of the west coast, with glimpses of the Manukau Harbour and its heads to be seen from some of the cafes in buildings in the Titirangi village, buildings such as Lopdell House, an Art Deco structure that opened in 1930 as the Hotel Titirangi, and eventually became an arts centre.

In front of Lopdell House is a statue of a noted early Auckland environmentalist and water engineer, Henry Atkinson. Atkinson acquired much of the wilderness west of Auckland on his own account while laying out grand public waterworks in the same area, and then donated the surplus bush to Auckland for conservation purposes.[2]

Up a steep hill and never served by tram in the days when most people used trams to get around, Titirangi was once a notable artists' retreat – a bit like Heidelberg in Melbourne, for instance – and still has some of that vibe, as well as several rather Bohemian cafés, grand scenic views of the Manukau Harbour and a feeling of being on the edge of the bush: altogether, an ideal place to begin a nature ramble.

If you've seen the Victorian period drama *The Piano*, starring Holly Hunter, Anna Paquin and Harvey Keitel, this is the very area where most of it was filmed, and set. Auckland's wild west, battered by sea winds and spray from the Tasman Seal and dominated by hills and dunes covered in tough, leathery plants, is less touristy but at the same time more primeval than the east coast of the Auckland region, which is quite sheltered and faces the Pacific.

There are indeed few places so primordial and yet so close to a big city!

The mouth of the Pararaha Tunnel on the Piha tram line, with a group of workers standing beside the logging locomotive "Sandfly". Piha sawmill manager Mr H. P. Knutzen is seated on the front of the engine. Photographed by Albert Percy Godber between 1915 and 1916. A. P. Godber collection, Alexander Turnbull Library (Wellington), reference APG-0826-1/2-G.

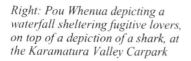

Right: Pou Whenua depicting a waterfall sheltering fugitive lovers, on top of a depiction of a shark, at the Karamatura Valley Carpark

Bottom: Manukau Heads, from north head hills near Huia

Manukau Heads as seen from the Omanawanui Track

The following photographs, and perhaps one or two of the preceding ones, were taken by a talented photographer whom I've enjoyed several hikes with, Nicki Botica Williams.

Whatipu-to-Karekare Coast

Scrambling over boulders in the Pararaha Gorge

Piha Beach and township with Lion Rock

Anawhata Beach

Anawhata Beach

Anawhata

Lake Wainamu from the south end, beach dunes at the north end

Te Henga Walkway, northward from Bethells Beach to Muriwai

Goldies Bush Track: Fern shoot

Goldies Bush Track: Mokoroa Falls

Muriwai

Muriwai: The Gannet Colony

An increasing number of tracks have been closed, and a rāhui or traditional ban proclaimed, to try and prevent the spread of kauri dieback disease in the Waitākere ranges. Visitors to the Waitākere should make themselves familiar with this issue. (Hopefully, a remedy will soon be found.) The best source of up-to-date information both about the trail in general, and also about which sections are open, is to be found on this Auckland Council link: **aucklandcouncil.govt.nz/parks-recreation/get-outdoors/Pages/hillary-trail.aspx**. If you are around locally, you can also visit the park rangers at Arataki Visitor Centre or call them on 09-817-0077.

Blog post with more images:

a-maverick.com/blog/aucklands-western-wilds

Reference Note

2 See 'Timespanner visits Titirangi Village' (19 June 2010), on the webpage timespanner.blogspot.co.nz/2010/06/timespanner-visits-titirangi-village.html. This link contains a number of attractive photographs.

TOUR 2: Coromandel, the Bay of Plenty and East Cape

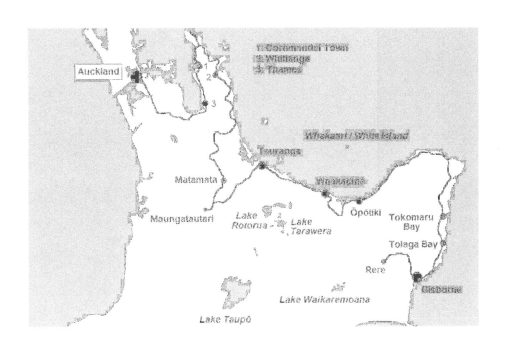

CHAPTER THIRTEEN

Cruising around the Coromandel

THE COROMANDEL PENINSULA sits east of Auckland, on the far side of the Hauraki Gulf. Generally known just as the Coromandel for short, the peninsula's not really on the way to anywhere else. So, you have to make a special trip. And it's really rugged, mostly covered in forested mountains with a low density of population.

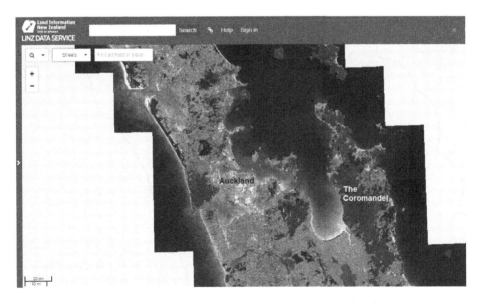

New Zealand ten-metre satellite imagery, *from Land Information New Zealand (LINZ), accessed 16 July 2020, with names of Auckland and The Coromandel added for this book. LINZ content is CC-BY-4.0.*

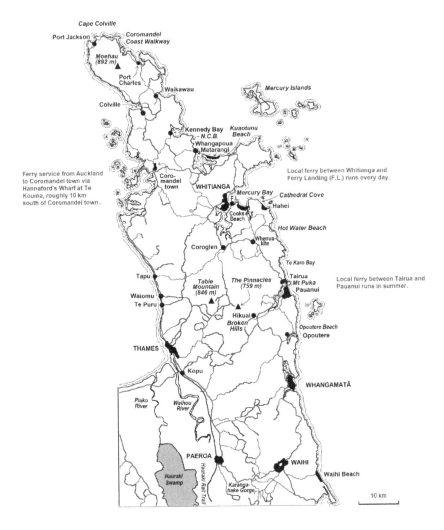

Closer Map of the Coromandel Peninsula. *The green lines are the main tramping tracks, and the red lines are a selection of the local roads, with an emphasis on roads that lead to trail ends and to the marked destinations. The purple line is the Hauraki Rail Trail for cyclists (marked). N.C.B., near Whangapoua, is New Chums Beach. Not every township or locality is shown, and some tracks shown may also have been closed to limit the spread of Kauri Dieback Disease.*

All of which makes the Coromandel a top holiday destination and hippie hangout! The more so, because the peninsula is really scenic, with a ton of lonely beaches and offshore islands, as well as inland tramping tracks. In fact, the population on the peninsula can soar past a hundred and thirty thousand in summer as holidaymakers descend on the region, mostly from Auckland.

As we head toward the Coromandel, its exotic, jungly mountains loom larger and larger, including the Coromandel Pinnacles, the subject of the next chapter.

There's a whole network of tramping tracks on the peninsula and all sorts of things to do on the coast, including surfing. Surf beaches include Waikawau Beach, Kuaotunu Beach, New Chums Beach, Whitianga (two spots), Hot Water Beach, Te Karo Bay, Tairua, and Whangamatā Beach. There are competitions held at Whitianga and Whangamatā.

And there are scenic beaches as well like Cathedral Cove and New Chums (both scenery and surf), and, of course, the spa bathing opportunities presented by the volcanic Hot Water Beach in addition to the surf. Or, you can just go fishing.

The Islands of Whangamatā

There is also clear water for diving, since the Coromandel's rivers mostly run pure through the forest. And the peninsula's got a lot of off-the-beaten-track character too.

Check out the local tourism website, **TheCoromandel.com**. This is quite simply the best tourist website I've ever seen, complete with drone flyovers, and tells you a lot more than I could, including all campsites and freedom camping sites. There's also a Coromandel app that you can download for Android and Apple devices.

You shouldn't confuse such information sources with **Coromandel.com**, which sells deep-storage batteries to the local off-grid hippies. Of whom there are also quite a few. In fact, a lot of the Coromandel has a sort of countercultural look. Many people have signs up opposed to mining.

And that's because, along with the pillaging of the local forests, mining used to be the economic lifeblood of the

Coromandel. There's still a big gold mine in Waihi, the Martha pit, which the town is organised around like a ring.

Another downtown attraction in Waihi is the Cornish Pumphouse. It once housed machinery used for dewatering the local gold mine. The old pumphouse was moved to its present site in 2006 in a feat of modern engineering, being slid 300 metres on Teflon-coated bearers.

The Cornish Pumphouse in Waihi once housed machinery used for dewatering the local gold mine, which still produces gold to this day.

Well worth a visit, also, is the derelict mining area in the nearby Karangahake Gorge.

__Old Mining track on the southern side of the Karangahake Gorge,__ which joins to the 'Windows Walk' via the bridge shown. Public domain photograph by Ingolfson, January 2011, via Wikimedia Commons.

The mining era began with a gold rush in 1868, and to this day even Thames, the biggest town in the region with a population of 7,000, has something of a Wild West look, the date 1868 stencilled above a number of hastily-erected and now-historic buildings.

Adding to the atmosphere is the fact that you can buy everything you need to make moonshine in the local shops, this being perfectly legal in New Zealand (and just about nowhere else). You're in *The Luminaries* country here, basically.

The peninsula is volcanic, and that is why it's rich in minerals. The two tend to go together as volcanic process bring up minerals from deep under the earth and concentrate them near the surface.

The volcanoes of the peninsula are millions of years old and considered to be well-extinct, but there's still some residual heat. On the east coast of the Coromandel, near Whitianga, there's a place called Hot Water Beach. If you time it right you can dig out a hole on the beach, have it fill with seawater percolating through the sands and relax in a hot bath.

Another major attraction near Whitianga is Cathedral Cove, where erosion has carved a cave into the shape of a gothic cathedral and created other weird-looking rocks.

In the summer it's a one-and-a-quarter hour walk from a carpark at Hahei, which is really nice in itself, and in winter a 45 minute walk from a lookout where you can't park in summer. Hahei is a shortened version of the Māori name for Mercury Bay, Te Whanganui-a-Hei.

One of the best ways to do Cathedral Cove is actually by boat. You can even do a glass-bottomed boat tour.

Just north of Whitianga there's also a really lonesome beach with no signs of development anywhere nearby that you have to take a track to, called New Chums.

In fact, if you mainly want to do beach and coastal stuff, the area around Whitianga, including the more suburban Cooks Beach, is hard to beat.

As to my itinerary this July, I started out from Thames, where my dad lives, and travelled more or less clockwise around the peninsula. I started out by exploring the funky Thames markets.

Then I went north along the coast to Waiomu, where there is a coast walk through kauri forests to the east coast of the peninsula as well as entry to a network of tracks that leads to the Pinnacles. It's important to note that some tracks through kauri forests may be closed because of the spread of Kauri Dieback Disease, however, so do check this first before making plans!

There was a beach cafe but no petrol station at Waiomu; the nearest one was at Tapu. There were people fishing, and cormorants diving for fish as well.

Then I travelled north to Coromandel town halfway up the west coast of the peninsula. Coromandel town is where you can arrive by ferry from Auckland. I think that an ideal way to explore the Coromandel would be to take an EBike over on the ferry from Auckland!

Coromandel town is famous for its picturesque appearance and generally laid-back quality. There are also lots of bushwalks nearby.

While I was at Coromandel town I visited the Driving Creek Railway, a bush tramway built by the late potter Barry Brickell, and also hiked the Kauri Block Track to the Pā Lookout (Pā means Māori village) which has great views over Coromandel town's harbour (with more islands!)

You can head further north through Colville, where there is the Mahamudra Buddhist centre, and on to the tip of the peninsula with Mount Moehau, Waikawau and the coastal walkways.

Then I came back and turned east to go to Matarangi and Kuaotunu Beach and then down through Whitianga to Coroglen and from there to Hot Water Beach.

And Cathedral Cove. Well, almost to Cathedral Cove as I suddenly realised that I was running short of time. Here's a photo I got off Facebook – I think you should make the effort to get to Cathedral Cove, after all!

A good place to stay on the Coromandel, if you are going to be based on one spot, is Whenuakite, which is quite central and cheaper than other places. It's pronounced fenua - kitay, roughly speaking, not kite as on a string.

I carried on down through Tairua, with its pinnacle-like Mount Puka, to Hikuai where I visited the Broken Hills Campsite. This is another industrial archaeology area, with lots of walking tracks as well. From Hikuaui, you get to the Broken Hills area via the Puketui Valley Road.

And then on to Opoutere where a friend of mine lives, and visited the nearby beach.

On the way back to Thames I went by way of State Highway 25A. There are some lovely walks directly off this highway. Puketui Road, which is another way of getting to Broken Hills, also comes off State Highway 25A roughly in the middle. You can't drive right through Broken Hills to the Puketui *Valley* Road, which I mentioned on the previous page. You can only come in from either end.

In the southern part of the peninsula and the plains to the southwest you also get good views of Table Mountain.

Yes, Table Mountain. It isn't as well-known as its South African namesake, but only because Coromandel's a bit off the beaten track, unlike Cape Town.

Like the Table Mountain in South Africa, the Coromandel's Table Mountain is home to a variety of rare plants that grow on the plateau on top.

TABLE MOUNTAIN, A WELL-KNOWN PICTURESQUE LANDSCAPE BETWEEN THAMES AND MERCURY BAY, AUCKLAND.　　　F. Causley, Photo.

Table Mountain or Whakairi (Coromandel), photographed by F. Causley, published in the supplement to the 'Auckland Weekly News', 28 September 1905, p. 14. Auckland Libraries Heritage Collections AWNS-19050928–14–3, no known copyright.

Such a prominent feature also has a Māori name, naturally. This is Te Kohatu-whakairi-a-Ngatoroirangi, meaning the Upraised Rock of Ngatoroirangi, the priestly navigator of the waka or voyaging canoe Te Arawa, said to have brought the ancestors of the Arawa people to New Zealand: the land that would later be known in Māori as Aotearoa. The short form of the name is Whakairi, meaning Upraised.

There's an article about the Coromandel's Table Mountain in *New Zealand Wilderness Magazine,* which even includes a photo of the Table Mountain, or Whakairi, complete with a white 'tablecloth' cloud: just the sort of thing to make Cape Town dwellers homesick.

Whakairi is a bit hard to get to even on foot, the Department of Conservation being in no hurry to improve access and thus endanger its rare plants. The *New Zealand Wilderness Magazine* article asks whether an ascent of this mountain is, in fact, New Zealand's worst tramp. But you can still admire it from afar.

Blog post with more images:

a-maverick.com/blog/cruising-around-the-coromandel-by-road-in-new-zealand

CHAPTER FOURTEEN

The Pinnacles: hundreds of steps in rock

MY MOTHER fell in love with the Kauaeranga Valley near Thames on the Coromandel Peninsula, and decided to move there from Hastings in 1980. I did heaps of walks in the area right through the '80s and into the '90s.

I tramped the Coromandel Pinnacles Walk, also called the Kauaeranga Kauri Trail, for the first time in the 1980s and have since done it about ten times since.

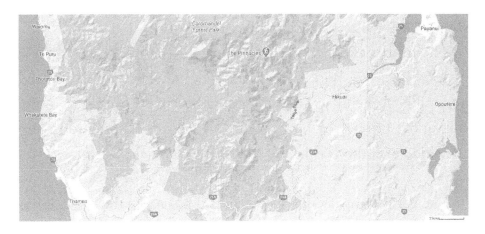

The Pinnacles are top centre in this area of the lower Coromandel Peninsula, the Firth of Thames left. *Map data ©2020 Google.*

> The website **thecoromandel.com** has a page on the Pinnacles among its must-does, and this is a good information source: **thecoromandel.com/activities/must-do/the-pinnacles.**

The track up to the Pinnacles is not especially difficult for a fit person, as it was carved into the form of a staircase (in the steeper sections) so that kauri loggers, miners, and kauri gum diggers, excavating the ground for unfossilised resin, could get pack horses up and down.

The Pinnacles summit is only 759 metres high. Still, the track is quite steep in places, above all on the Pinnacles themselves. The Pinnacles are the hard cores of eroded volcanoes: a fact which accounts for their steepness. Just below the summit, the Pinnacles are fitted with climbing ladders.

The nearby Pinnacles Hut sleeps eighty people. Even so, it is a good idea to book ahead in view of the popularity and accessibility of this walk. Many people of all ages walk up to the hut all the time, even if they have no intention of venturing up the ladders all the way to the top of the Pinnacles.

The Kauaeranga Valley is a beautiful place. All the same, it has seen a lot of extractive industry. In addition to logging, mining used to be a mainstay of the local economy, and gold mining has started up again lately. Both my family and many of the other residents in the area want it to stop because it's very polluting to the natural landscape of the valley.

Climbing up to the Pinnacles via the old pack-horse route created by miners, kauri loggers and kauri gum diggers in the early 1900s

This is incredible... we should reach the top in under an hour

On the edge. The view is so worth it.

Blog post with more images:

a-maverick.com/blog/the-coromandel-pinnacles-of-new-zealand-hundreds-of-steps-in-rock

CHAPTER FIFTEEN

The Kaimai: Mount Te Aroha and Wairere Falls, with a side trip to Hobbiton

I'VE done Mount Te Aroha twice. At 952 metres, it's the highest peak in the Kaimai-Mamaku Range, which continues the mountains of the Coromandel Peninsula southward, next to the Hauraki Plains.

Mount Te Aroha is located next to the spa town of Te Aroha, halfway along the Kaimai Range. The climb isn't challenging, and it takes only three hours to reach the summit if you are reasonably fit. There are lots of other tracks nearby.

On the facing page, there's a map of the Hauraki Rail Trail cycleway I saw in Matamata, south of Te Aroha. The map shows where both Te Aroha and Matamata are in relation to the Kaimai Range. They are accessible by road too, of course.

A highlight of Mount Te Aroha is the group of hot springs at the foot of the mountain. These springs have been used for hundreds of years for their healing properties.

In the late 1800s the land was gifted to New Zealand by the Māori chief Mokena Hou to be used as a public health resort, and has remained a popular spot for bathers ever since. There are many other hot springs in the Waikato area and the wider North Island, and some in the South Island as well.

133

Typical Mount Te Aroha terrain

View from the top of Mount Te Aroha, with the Pacific Ocean in the distance

The other highlight of the Kaimai Range, a little south of Mount Te Aroha, is the Wairere Falls. Wairere Falls are 153 metres high and visible from the Wairere Falls Carpark, about 25 km south of the town of Te Aroha on State Highway 27.

Wairere Falls, photo by C. Rodliffe, 21 March 2008, CC-BY-3.0 via Wikimedia Commons

There's quite a pleasant hike up to Wairere Falls from the carpark, with a picturesque bridge and lots of other photo opportunities.

See the Department of Conservation PDF brochure *Family walks in the Waikato*. Also waikatonz.com (web resource), *Te Aroha Mineral Springs* and the websites for the privately-owned Opal Hot Springs Holiday Park and Okoroire Hot Springs. A comprehensive list of hot pools in any locality is provided by **nzhotpools.co.nz.**

The falls are close to Matamata, where the Hobbiton™ film set from the *Lord of the Rings* films is located.

A Selfie by the Hobbiton sign

For tours of Hobbiton, visit the website of Hobbiton Movie Set Tours. It's all still pretty much as it was in the *Lord of the Rings* movies.

Hobbiton cost me NZ $90 to get in when I visited (the price varies with the season), but the ticket was well worth it! The movie set verges onto the streets of Matamata, rather incongruously. Then again, if all our country towns were like this, they might be a bit more pleasant.

It's better to go in the morning because things get rather crowded in the afternoon. You can book online for an early morning tour. And while the cost of entry may seem steep it also means that the numbers are limited, in the morning at any rate. You're able to take photos and videos. The Green Dragon pub is the highlight: it's fully furnished inside. In the blog post associated with this chapter, there's a video I made of Hobbiton outdoors, followed by a scene in a blacksmith's, and then inside the Green Dragon.

Other interesting places to visit in the vicinity are Okoroire some 18 kilometres distant in a southward direction, where the hot springs hotel has been in operation since the 1880s; and the much chillier Blue Spring, a further 12 kilometres on near Putaruru, which supplies about 60 per cent of New Zealand's bottled water. Both of these are up back roads, so check your GPS.

There's a backpackers' hostel just outside of Matamata, where you can base yourself if you don't want to stay somewhere else, such as the Okoroire Hot Springs Hotel.

Once you've detoured this far, you might as well detour just a little further southwest to Maungatautari, the Sanctuary Mountain, which is the subject of the next chapter.

Blog post with more images:

a-maverick.com/blog/the-kaimai-range-of-new-zealand-from-mount-te-aroha-to-hobbiton

CHAPTER SIXTEEN

The Sanctuary Mountain

T HE largest ecological reserve so far enclosed by a pest-proof barrier fence, anywhere in the world, can be found south-west of Matamata, at Maungatautari Reserve.

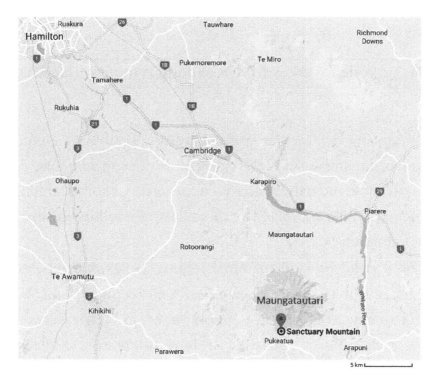

The overall location of Maungatautari and its tourism facility, *indicated as 'Sanctuary Mountain' at the southern end of the Maungatautiri Reserve. Map data ©2019 Google, name 'Maungatautari' added for this map.*

Maungatautari has been a nature reserve since 1912. The decision to fence it off came after the discovery of several rare species hiding in its rugged terrain, indicating that it was more significant than some other nature reserves. These included a population of the silver birch, an ice-age survivor thought to have died out entirely in the North Island, and a new population of Hochstetter's frogs, a rare and ancient species confined to New Zealand.

The website for the reserve is **sanctuarymountain.co.nz**.

By fencing off the reserve it became possible to eliminate introduced mammals and thus prevent further species loss. And, even, to allow the natural ecosystem to recover something of its former glory. New Zealand's ecosystems evolved in the absence of land mammals.

The control of land mammals.–. cats, stoats, weasels, dogs, rabbits, rats, mice, goats, sheep, deer, and so on.–. is absolutely central to any ecological restoration project in New Zealand.

I saw North Island robins, stitchbirds, saddlebacks and fantails, as well as kākā, the large forest parrots that are cousins of the more famous, alpine kea.

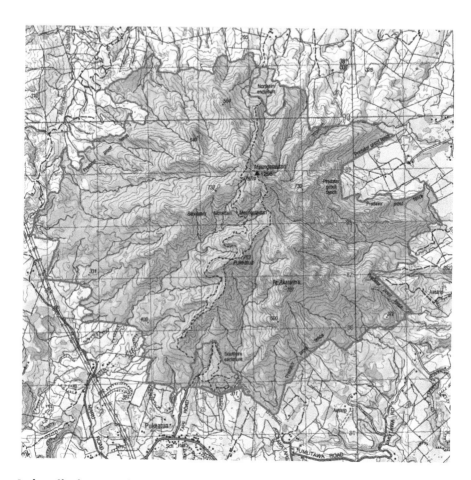

A detailed map of Mangatautari showing the 47 km pest-proof fence around the whole mountain and the Northern and Southern enclosures, highlighted in red for this map. *The Tautari Wetland is to the southwest of the Southern Enclosure. The boundary and fence details are out of date in the area southwest of the Southern Enclosure, not yet reflecting the gift of land from a farm owned by the Tauroa family around the small pond shown. Map data by LINZ via NZ Topo Map, 2019.*

A kākā feeding on spring buds in the Wellington Botanic Gardens.
Photo by Kate Macbeth (2018), CC-BY-SA 4.0, via Wikimedia Commons.

This time, we were especially looking for fungi (mushrooms and toadstools, and their relatives). There are thousands of species of fungi in New Zealand, many of them native to damp and dripping forests like those of Maungatautari. In fact, if we were to come across any extra-weird mushrooms or toadstools, or ones completely new to science, Maungatautari would be the place to find them.

Maungatautari scenes from our trip, mostly of fungi

We went up the wooden lookout tower for a look, naturally enough. It only took twenty people and had been built by volunteers. It swayed in the wind, but you got a bird's-eye view of the forest canopy.

At the tower, we saw more kākā, which the staff encouraged to arrive by shaking bird feeders. There wasn't any food in the feeders yet but the kākā turned up all the same, knowing there soon would be.

The reserve includes a 'tuatarium', home to the prehistoric tuatara that I've mentioned earlier in the chapter on Tiritiri Matangi, where they also thrive: an ancient reptile which looks a bit like an iguana but is from a much older lineage dating back some 220 million years.

'Henry', a 100 year old-plus tuatara at the Southland Museum and Art Gallery in Invercargill, in 2007. Photo by KeresH, CC-BY-3.0, via Wikimedia Commons.

The large blue flightless takahē, once nearly extinct, also now thrives on the margins of the wetland.

In the wetland we also saw kōura, or freshwater crayfish. It was pretty exceptional to see that, as kōura are another rare species that has mostly died out in New Zealand outside of places like Maungatautari. I took photos of kōura in the water, but it was muddy and I didn't have a polarising filter, so they didn't really come out. Instead, here's one from a display:

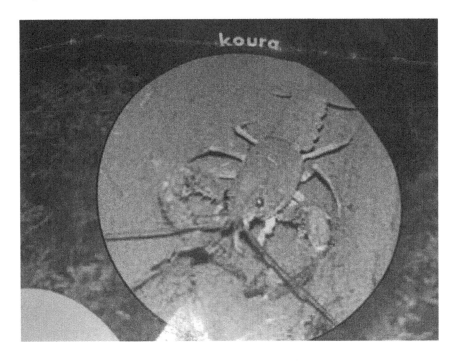

In the next chapter, the tour continues over the Kaimai Range and on around East Cape.

Blog post with more images:

a-maverick.com/blog/the-sanctuary-mountain

CHAPTER SEVENTEEN

From Tauranga to Gisborne: A slow journey around New Zealand's East Cape

THE East Cape's got a long coastline with lots of beaches, and yet it's also 'off the beaten track' even for tourists: which is perhaps getting close to a unique combination in today's world. It's a really good place to visit if you want to have an unpressured sort of a holiday. Just two weeks by the seaside in a small hotel or cabin or under the canvas of a big old tent listening to the booming surf in your bunk at night. The kind of holiday a lot of New Zealanders had as kids and remember all their lives.

The East Cape is also an area with strong Māori traditions, as old-time European settlers also left it alone for the most part. In Māori the region is known as Tairāwhiti, which means almost the same thing, namely, 'East Side'.

A good guide to the East Cape or Tairāwhiti region is **exploretheeastcape.co.nz**, which includes a free online ebook. And you can get printed tourism maps and fliers along the way as well, which are probably more convenient to use in the car.

The first part of the journey is along the sweeping, sandy shores of the Bay of Plenty or Te Moana-a-Toi (the Sea of Toi,

149

an ancestral navigator), where there are two sizable towns, Whakatāne and Ōpōtiki.

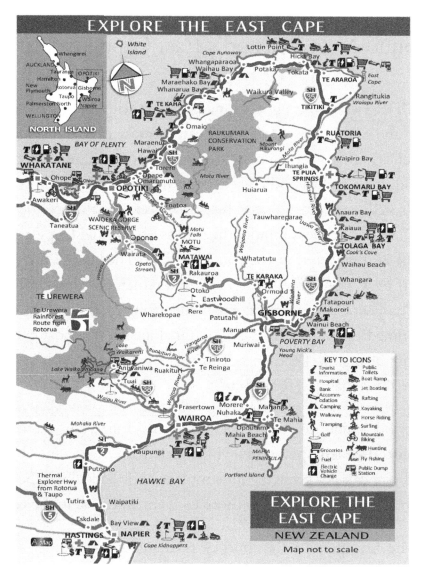

Map courtesy of ABMaps and Explore the East Cape *Guide,* **exploretheeastcape.co.nz**

After Ōpōtiki the coast of the cape itself is quite rugged and there are no big towns, just villages, until you get to Gisborne, which is actually quite a long way to go. It pays to keep well gassed up.

Gisborne is located in a bay officially called Tūranganui-a-Kiwa / Poverty Bay. The Māori name means the great (or long) standing-place of <u>Kiwa</u>, an ancestral hero or demigod associated with the ocean. The Pacific Ocean is sometimes called Te Moana-nui a Kiwa, the great sea of Kiwa.

Mount Maunganui

The English names Bay of Plenty and Poverty Bay also demand explanation. They were bestowed by Captain Cook, who was impressed by the fertile shores of the Sea of Toi and disappointed by a failure to obtain provisions in the long-standing-place of Kiwa. Yet Poverty Bay is also quite fertile. Even Captain Cook didn't get everything right.

After Tauranga and Mount Maunganui, along the shores of Te Moana-a -Toi, you come to Whakatāne.

There is a huge rock in the middle of Whakatāne called Pōhatuora which has been consecrated as a war memorial. It sits in the middle of a town square, in a way that's shown in the photo on this page. Pōhatuora makes it fairly easy to find your way around.

There are amazing light-show experiences at the Mataatua Marae which you can take in for as little as NZ $15. The Mataatua Marae is also famous for having a meeting-house which has travelled around the world, on display and residing in anthropological museums in Australia and Britain for more than 130 years before being repatriated to Aotearoa (the Māori name for New Zealand) and re-erected!

Mataatua

Whakatāne offers all kinds of wilderness and tourism experiences including walks and overnight stays in the Whirinaki rainforest and a visit to the Muriwai Caves. There are also several historic pā including the Pā of Toi on the Nga Tapuwae o Toi, or The Footsteps of Toi, walkway.

Being open to the northern sun, and sheltered from southerly winds, is important for the cultivation of the kūmara. In local lore, a female hero named Hinehākirirangi brought the first kūmara from the tropical Pacific islands in the 1300s by the European calendar.

After first being shipwrecked in the Ōhiwa lagoon, Hinehākirirangi made her home at the Muriwai Cave at Whakatāne for a time and planted kūmara all around the region.

The Muriwai Cave at Whakatāne

Whakaari / White Island: The former tourist destination

Whakatāne is the town from which people used to set out to go to Whakaari / White Island. I doubt that these tours will resume but they haven't had time to change the signs yet.

Located eighty minutes off the coast from Whakatāne in the Bay of Plenty, the remote Whakaari or White Island is New Zealand's most active volcano. Despite this, many visitors were drawn to the island for its natural beauty and geothermal activity, as well as the abundance of marine life near the island, until an eruption in 2019 led to major loss of life.

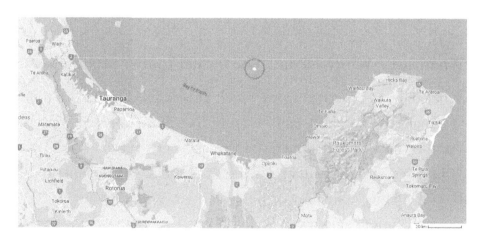

Whakaari / White Island, indicated by a circle, in the Bay of Plenty. Map Data ©2020 Google.

The island contains large amounts of sulfur which in the past was mined for making acid, fertiliser, and industrial chemicals. Sulfurous minerals, dissolved in groundwater, also run into the sea off in the form of a natural chemical plume which is toxic near the island but which has a fertilising effect on the sea life as it becomes diluted, further out.

Whakaari / White Island, with steaming crater and boiling mud pools

An eruption in 1914 killed all the miners on the island. Only their cat survived, as it was able to find a place to hide. Despite that grim precedent, the island became a tourist destination in recent years, until tragedy struck once more in 2019.

There are other volcanoes in New Zealand that are quite active as well. The largest, Mount Ruapehu, has skifields on its flanks.

What makes Whakaari / White Island different is that not only is it even more active but also it is an undersea volcano, so that the bit that pokes out of the water is the very top, the constantly active crater area.

On Mount Ruapehu a skier is normally miles from the crater and in little danger from any eruption unless it is huge, in which case there would be enough advance warning in the form of earthquakes, and so on, to close the ski-fields.

The last time there were big eruptions on Mount Ruapehu, in 1995 and 1996, the ski-fields were closed in plenty of time.

But smaller eruptions occur with less warning. These incur little danger on Ruapehu but have twice proven to be killers on Whakaari / White Island, where about half of the island is actually taken up by the crater.

Visiting Whakaari / White Island for mere tourism was always a bad idea and I don't think it will ever re-open.

East past the Marshes

East of Whakatāne I drove around Ōhiwa Harbour, an ecologically important lagoon with two sandspits guarding it from the sea, Ōhope and Ōhiwa. Both are popular beach resorts, and I visited the Onekawa Marae at Ōhiwa.

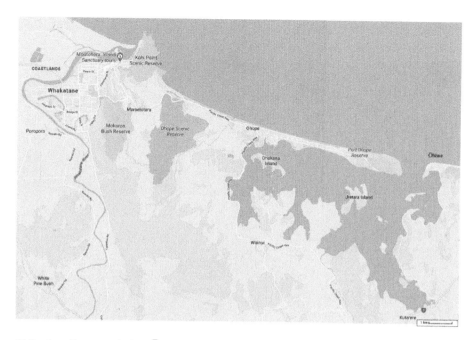

Whakatāne and the Ōhiwa Lagoon. *The name of Ōhiwa township has been added for the purpose of this book. Background map data ©2020 Google.*

Soon afterward, you come to Ōpōtiki. There's the option, there, of a turn off to an inland road to Gisborne via the spectacular Waioeka Gorge, but I pressed on round the cape.

A gateway welcoming travellers to the Whānau-ā-Apanui rohe
(territory) on State Highway 35, the main coast road along the Bay of
Plenty and around East Cape

The condition of the coastal road was variable and there were slips in places, due to heavy rain that dogged me on the whole trip.

In fact, I only just made it through before State Highway 35 was closed.

'Mighty Mōtū': The last untamed river in the North Island

A big attraction for trampers and boaties, once you get past Ōpōtiki, is the Mōtū River, which enters the sea at Maraenui, and the Mōtū Trails which partly run alongside. These trails form a loop that goes far into the mountains and then back out again.

161

The Mōtū's sometimes called the Mighty Mōtū, as it's a really wild river full of high – grade rapids and waterfalls that attract daring kayakers and rafters for a distance of 100km up from the river's mouth. You can also go up and down the Mōtū by jetboat if you don't feel quite so brave, physical, or keen on getting soaked.

The Mouth of the Mōtū at Maraenui with the bridge carrying the coastal highway, State Highway 35, behind

Every other big river in the North Island has had rapids blown up, been dammed, had water taken for hydroelectricity or irrigation, or been subjected to flood-control measures at the insistence of local farmers and townsfolk. The Mōtū is the only big river on the island that is still completely 'wild'. It cascades through a total wilderness for most of its length including the final stretches, and nothing's been done to tame it.

Decorated Gates

Māori culture is famous for its decorative arts. I was just blown away by the fabulous carving at many of the marae, or meeting houses, of the Bay of Plenty and the Tairāwhiti region.

One of my favourites was Whitianga Marae, near the Mōtū River mouth, which has an amazing gate-carving or waharoa and an equally amazing memorial to 2nd Lt Te-Moana-nui-a-Kiwa Ngārimu, one of two Māori to have won the Victoria Cross (VC), the British equivalent of America's Medal of Honor. I've got a big photo of this gate on the next page.

Traditionally, mountains were seen as the abode of the gods. The highest and most prominent local peak in the East Cape region is Mount Hikurangi, a correspondingly sacred mountain from which some of the earliest sun rays of the new millennium were broadcast around the world.

Mount Hikurangi, photographed by Phillip Capper (14 December 2010), CC-BY-2.0 via Wikimedia Commons

My cultural journey around East Cape included a visit to St Mary's Church at Tikitiki, which was built in the 1920s as a memorial to Māori soldiers and other personnel who served in World War One. It was a masterful achievement, restored in the early 2000s.

165

An article in *New Zealand Geographic* describes it as "the gift and inspiration of Sir Āpirana Ngata," one of the most prominent Māori leaders, politicians and modernisers of the first half of the twentieth century along with the anthropologist Te Rangi Hiroa, also known as Sir Peter Buck. Ngata used building projects like Tikitiki to revitalize Māori crafts and also to remind Māori that they weren't fading away in the face of European colonization, as some supposed they might.

Sir Āpirana Ngata leading the Haka at Waitangi, north of Auckland, in the Treaty of Waitangi Centennial celebrations, 6 February 1940. Photograph by Bert Snowden, National Library of New Zealand, Tiaki reference 1/2–029794-F.

Further round the cape, I visited Te Puia Springs, healing springs where there is a hospital now run by the health board of the Ngati Porou Iwi, Ngati Porou Hauora, which Te Ara, the online encyclopaedia of New Zealand, describes as "the principal health provider on the East Coast."

Te Puia Springs is also a resort that anyone can visit, with an old and traditional-looking wooden hotel which is supposed to be haunted by a ghost, as well as a more modern motel.

All in all, the Māori lore and history of this region is basically limitless. There is a useful website called **Tupapa.nz** which also comes with an app.

Further Ramblings

At Te Araroa, I saw a Pohutukawa tree said to be New Zealand's oldest and biggest, Te Waha o Rerekohu, 600 years old, 21.2m tall and 40m wide.

I came across information about whales, including a grave where more than fifty sperm whales were buried after an epic stranding of these huge creatures.

And many freedom camping sites.

A cross-looking guardian warns off interlopers who would injure the ancient, almost shapeless tree Te Waha o Rerekohu by climbing on it

I eventually arrived in Tokomaru Bay, the site of an old (meat-) freezing works, now a piece of industrial archaeology.

I used to come here as a kid. There are old baches (or cabins), and a famously long wharf which now needs restoring.

At Tokomaru Bay I met a café proprietor named Rachel whose business was on leased Māori land. She was trying to sell the café for NZ $250,000 with 29 years still to run. She quipped that her pāua (abalone) pies, which get rave reviews online, earn a thousand dollars a minute in summer!

Tolaga Bay has a wharf that's even longer than the Tokomaru Bay wharf. In fact, it's the longest wharf in New Zealand, 660 metres in total. Unlike the wharf at Tokomaru Bay, this wharf has been restored. Such long wharves date back to the days when local roads were very poor, so that direct shipping was the only way to get large amounts of produce in and out.

According to one account of the Tolaga Bay wharf, from the website **newzealand.com**,

"It was ironic that much of the cargo that passed over the wharf was road-making material, used to construct the road through to Gisborne, soon providing an alternate means of transport."

At Tolaga Bay there's also the Cooks Cove Walk. The area is called Cooks Cove because Captain Cook pulled in here during his first voyage to New Zealand, in 1769. The voyage was massively commemorated on its 200th anniversary in 1969, though commemoration has been more controversial on the 250th anniversary in 2019.

I headed through to Gisborne fairly quickly because of heavy rain that had dogged my trip so far. But not without noticing logs and wood waste from forestry operations washed into the sea at Tolaga Bay, a local eco-scandal that is making the beach unusable.

The area near Gisborne was also the base of operations of Te Kooti, a charismatic guerilla leader who resisted European colonisers in the aftermath of the extensive confiscation of Māori lands in the 1860s. Te Kooti founded a sect called Ringatū, meaning upraised hand, which still exists to this day. In a blog post, I describe how Te Kooti was arrested and exiled to the Chatham Islands, before making his escape once more.

Portrait of Te Kooti*, believed authentic and possibly a police photograph, donated to the Gisborne Museum by a Mrs Shaw, who said that it was in the possession of her father since at least 1873*

Te Kooti is the main inspiration for the character of Te Wheke in the 1983 epic *Utu* ('just deserts'), which has lately been remastered as *Utu Redux*. You can see the whole of the old version for free on Youtube.

173

Just before you get to Gisborne there is a marine reserve at Pouawa Beach.

Gisborne: Waka Prow sculpture

There's a whole heap of things to do in and around Gisborne, including feeding stingrays (!) at Tatapouri and doing a natural luge at Rere.

Blog post with more images:

a-maverick.com/blog/from-hobbiton-to-rocket-lab-a-slow-journey-around-new-zealands-east-cape

TOUR 3: The Historic Waikato

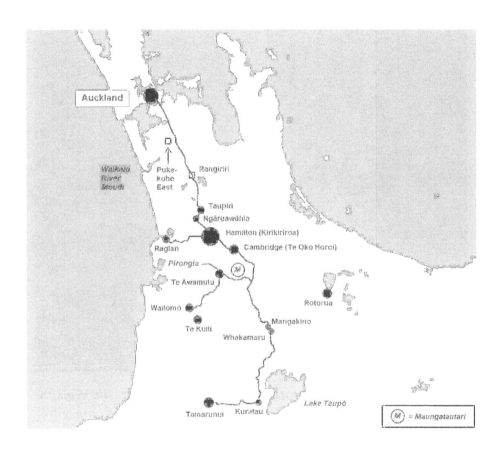

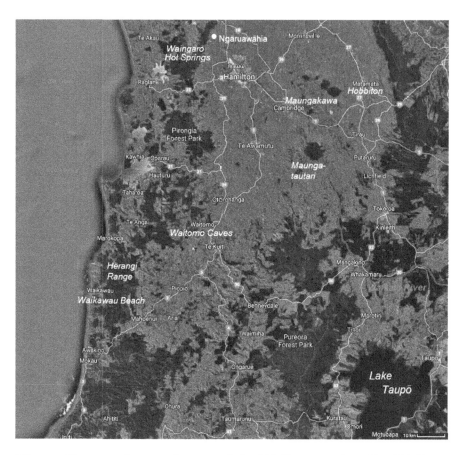

The southern and central parts of the Waikato region. *The Waikato River is shown in blue for this book. Taumarunui is at bottom centre. The names of Lake Taupō, Waikawau Beach, Hērangi Range, Waikato River, Waitomo Caves, Maungatautari, Maungakawa, Hobbiton, Ngāruawāhia and Waingaro Hot Springs have all been added for this book. Background imagery ©2020 Landsat/Copernicus, Data SIO, NOAA, U. S. Navy, NGA, GEBCO, TerraMetrics. Background map data ©2020 Google.*

CHAPTER EIGHTEEN

The Historic Waikato

THIS chapter is the first of three about my journey into and through the lands of New Zealand's longest river, the Waikato, which flows for 425 km from Lake Taupō down to the sea through the Waikato plains.

My starting point for this journey was Taumarunui, on the Whanganui River. Taumarunui is an old Māori settlement that evolved into a town in more recent times, first as a terminus for Whanganui riverboats.

From Taumarunui you can head northeast to the Pureora Forest Park, west of Lake Taupo. Pureora is in the geographical centre of the North Island.

For those on the road, there's also a lookout over Lake Taupo and the volcanoes of the central North Island at the Waituhi saddle.

If you take that road, you can turn left at Kuratau and carry on up State Highway 32, west of Lake Taupo. There are several tracks and local roads leading to tracks in the Pureora Forest Park that come off to the left as you head north on SH 32.

Eventually you'll come to the Waikato River at Whakamaru, the site of one of the Waikato's eight dams. Via Waipapa Road you get to another dam at Maraetai, and then via other roads to the Arapuni Dam.

If you go back toward the river and carry on you get to Karapiro, another artificial lake where rowing championships are held, and the town of Cambridge.

Cambridge is located at the highest navigable point on the Waikato river, below Karapiro. To this day the town is surrounded by a 'town belt' of parkland, part of which is the relic of fortifications intended to fend off hostile Māori tribes, who were hostile because the town was built on confiscated land.

The monitor (armoured gunboat) **Pioneer** *doing battle with a Māori pā (fortification) at Meremere on 31 October 1863. Detail from an image catalogued as A-110–006 at the Alexander Turnbull Library, Wellington, via nzhistory.govt.nz.*

Both Cambridge and the larger nearby city of Hamilton, also on the Waikato river, were established on land confiscated from Waikato Māori, after their lands were invaded both overland and by way of the river.

The story of the invasion is told in a short clip from a 1990s TV series on the New Zealand wars, narrated by the historian James Belich. It's on **nzonscreen.com**. Here's a map of the northern part of the Waikato which originally appeared in James Cowan's *The New Zealand Wars* in the 1920s.

Cowan's map shows the location of Meremere, where the incident above took place, and also various other settlements, forts, battles and skirmishes in Auckland and the lower reaches of the Waikato River.

At Pukekohe East Church Stockade, one of the battle sites described in the map above, you can actually see bullet holes in an old wooden church and in the back of one of the gravestones in the churchyard, all dating back to September 1863.

There's an app that tells you much more about the history of the Waikato, on **heritage.org.nz/apps/the-waikato-war**.

Why was the Waikato invaded? The answer is simple: to get land.

New Zealand is generally thought of as a farming nation. But in reality, there isn't much good farmland in New Zealand.

In the whole of the country, it is only in the Waikato region, south of Auckland, that there is a large enough area of plains to present a flat inland horizon. And that's precisely why it was invaded.

New Zealand Topographical Map. Source: Gingko Maps, with four historic main port cities superimposed.

Indeed, it was Māori success in farming the region and supplying Auckland with essential supplies, even exporting rope to Britain, that prompted the invasion.

Māori Rope-making, circa 1903. *Hand coloured lantern slide, probably from the National Publicity Studios, Negative Number 1867. Archives reference: AAPG W3878 Box 1 / B21.*
archway.archives.govt.nz/ViewFullItem.do?code=2571278. *CC-BY-2.0* ***via*** *Archives New Zealand on Flickr.*

When the first Europeans arrived in New Zealand, they observed that the Māori were for the most part a settled, farming people.

On the other hand, the traditional crops that the ancestors of the Māori had brought from tropical Polynesia were hard to grow in New Zealand, a temperate country where most regions get frost in winter.

The tools, seeds and animals brought to New Zealand by the colonists were much more suited to local conditions and were soon adopted by the Māori in preference to their old way of doing things.

It was the Māori who showed that many parts of New Zealand could be farmed by British and European methods and would in fact yield bumper crops.

At which point, the claim was made that Auckland would never be safe unless the Māori behind the plough, on the verdant plains of the Waikato, were replaced by farmers of British stock! The fact that many Māori, including the Māori of the Waikato, had elected a Māori king in 1858 was taken as further proof of anti-settler intent.

In the next two chapters, I'll describe a visit to Pirongia mountain in the Waikato, and I'll then go on to describe further travels in the region in a chapter that links to a blog post describing visits to the famous Waitomo Caves, the battlefield of Rangiriri, and the still-existing Pukekohe East Church.

Blog post with more images:

a-maverick.com/blog/carrying-on-down-the-waikato-part-one

CHAPTER NINETEEN

Pirongia: A pretty subalpine climb in bog

THERE'S heaps of things for a visitor to the Waikato to do in the present day.

East of Cambridge, there's a range of low mountains with spectacular views over the plains and south to the volcanoes of the central North Island. You can drive to the top of Pukemako and look out from there. Further east, still just a few kilometres from Cambridge, are Hobbiton, Te Aroha Hot Springs, Mount Te Aroha and the Kaimai Range, all of which I've talked about in an earlier chapter.

West of Cambridge lie the town of Te Awamutu and Pirongia mountain, a subalpine mountain with beautiful granite rock faces.

In the remainder of this chapter, I'm going to talk about tramping on Pirongia which, at 959 metres high, is easily the highest peak in the Waikato region.

At only 25 kilometres southwest of Hamilton, the mountain is also the largest remaining area of native forest close to the Waikato's biggest city.

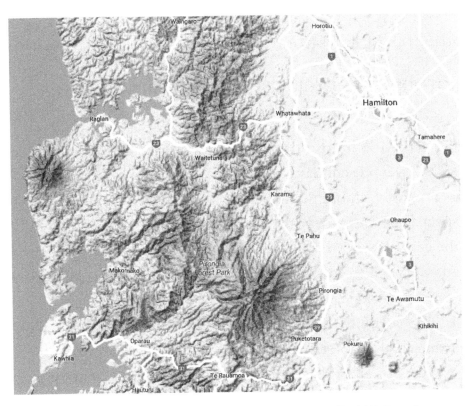

Pirongia, southwest of Hamilton. *Map Data ©2017 Google.*

Although there are several routes to the summit, when I tramped it we took the 18.5-kilometre-long Bell Track to the top, heading past the Kaniwhaniwha Caves and along a ridge to the Cone, which is the second-highest point on Mt Pirongia.

The Bell Track is very much up and down, as is the form of Mount Pirongia itself, so you will end up climbing a lot more than 959 metres in total: be warned! From the Cone, we carried on to the Pahautea Hut, where it's another thirty minutes to the summit.

Pirongia

The track itself forms part of the Waikato section of Te Araroa, meaning 'The Long Path', a trail that takes you the length of New Zealand all the way from Cape Rēinga to Bluff.

I tramped Pirongia in the summer and found that despite the heat, it was very muddy at the top.

The peaty soil grows beautiful subalpine ferns, and for anyone who is interested in ferns, Pirongia is a special treat.

Blog post with more images:

a-maverick.com/blog/pirongia-pretty-subalpine-climb-bog

CHAPTER TWENTY

More Waikato Adventures

SOUTH of Pirongia there's the Waitomo Caves, which are inhabited by creatures called glow-worms.

New Zealand glow-worms are carnivorous gnat larvae that live in caves in huge numbers. They hang sticky threads around themselves, lighting up the threads with a blue glow. Small creatures attracted by the light get tangled in the threads and devoured.

> Check out the official website of the Waitomo Caves Discovery Centre, on **waitomocaves.com.**

It's a pretty supernatural experience to be in a glow-worm cave. It's been called 'Avatar in real life'. I've also got some videos on a related blog post, linked at the end of this chapter.

If you head west from the Waitomo Caves, a journey on small roads through scenic country in the Hērangi Ranges, with other attractions along the way such as the Mangapohue Natural Bridge, leads eventually to Waikawau Beach, which you get to through a pedestrian tunnel.

This is in a really remote location, on a stretch of coast that doesn't have a road along it for 60 kilometres.

North of Pirongia mountain, which I wrote about in the last chapter, is Raglan: a township and harbour that attracts a lot of surfers and holidaymakers. The west coast of the North Island between Taranaki and Auckland is curiously uninhabited (or nearly so), and you can certainly get away from it all.

Raglan, 8 January 2011, photo by новичёк *(Novichok), CC-BY-3.0 via Wikimedia Commons.*

The most famous person to come from Raglan, most probably, is Eva Rickard, born Tuiawa Kereopa: a Māori woman who was given the name Eva in school, where speaking Māori and even the use of Māori names were forbidden in the belief that it would hold Māori pupils back.

And so Tuiawa was radicalised at about the age of five.

Tuiawa (Eva) Rickard dancing during the occupation of Moutoa Gardens, Whanganui, ca. 31 March 1995. Cropped detail from a full-length image taken by an unidentified Evening Post photographer. Photographic negatives and prints of the Evening Post and Dominion newspapers. Ref: EP/1995/0906/25. Alexander Turnbull Library, Wellington, New Zealand. The full-length image can be seen on /records/22748216

There are three world class surf breaks at Raglan and a surf school: in the North Island, there's a whole west coast surfing scene that extends down to Taranaki and up to the beaches west of Auckland such as Piha, where they have annual international surf championships.

From Raglan you can go due east on SH 23 to Hamilton, the largest inland city in New Zealand, with a population approaching 200,000.

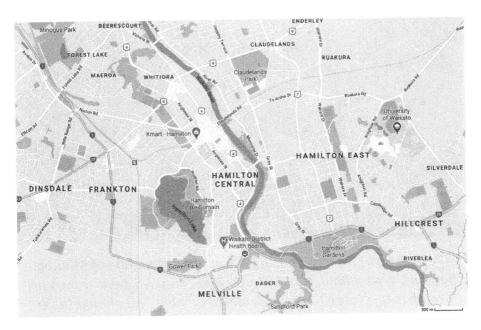

Hamilton. *Map data ©2020 Google.*

Like Cambridge, which is only a little way to its south, the city is cut in two by the Waikato River and has a string of bridges over the river, like the one you can just see at the right in the photo just above.

Hamilton has a generous endowment of parkland, including the amazing Hamilton Gardens, built on the site of a former rubbish dump on the banks of the river in the south-eastern part of the city.

The Hamilton Gardens are indeed plural, for there are twenty-one separate gardens including a Chinese scholar's garden and an Indian, Persian or Islamic garden in the square style divided by crossed paths which is known as Char Bagh, literally meaning 'four gardens'. You could spend a long time getting cheerfully lost in the Hamilton Gardens, which have been deliberately styled as a sort of wonderland. I always think that's the best sort of park!

The city is named after a British naval captain named John Fane Charles Hamilton who was killed at the Battle of Gate Pā near Tauranga in April 1864, some nine months after the invasion of the Waikato had begun. Hamilton and eight other officers had had dinner the night before in a house in Tauranga called the Elms, which still exists.

His last words were recorded as "follow me, men."

Hamilton is the only large city in New Zealand to have been built entirely on confiscated land, though one or two Auckland suburbs are as well, while many other urban centres in New Zealand have been built on land sold by Māori for a peppercorn sum in the earliest days of colonisation.

The Māori name for Hamilton, to which the city might well revert or become co-official in future in view of the obvious sensitivity of the confiscation issue, is Kirikiriroa, meaning a long stretch of gravel, sandbank or shingle bar.

Cambridge has three Māori names, Kemureti, Horotiu (an important historical pā) and Te Oko Horoi, the washbowl, a reference to the lake in the northern part of town, Lake Te Koo Utu or Te Koutu, where the second Māori King, Tāwhiao, symbolically washed his hands and face after the wars of the 1860s. The third of these names seems to be winning out as the preferred alternative to the colonial name. Horotiu has been applied to another locality nearby, so it would seem to be out of the running.

A statue of Captain Hamilton was erected as recently as 2013 in the city that bears his name, only to pulled down again in 2020 in deference to fast-changing sensibilities.

I took photos of pou, or totemic poles, outside the Sky City casino.

The Place to Stand

Just north of Hamilton or Kirikiriroa, at Ngāruawāhia, the Tūrangawaewae Marae is the centre of the Māori King movement, which once stood against the colonists with military force. The King was elected from 1858 onwards, to unify those Māori who were opposed to further British and settler encroachment on their lands, and who were prepared to fight if necessary. The institution exists to this day, in less warlike terms. There has been one reigning Māori Queen in the line, Te Atairangikaahu, who reigned from 1966 until 2006. The present Māori King bears the name of Tūheitia.

Tūrangawaewae means 'place to stand'. Ironically, these days, the complex has been visited by Queen Elizabeth II, as well as most of the members of her family. And all sorts of other famous people from overseas as well.

The King movement was based at Ngāruawāhia to begin with, until King Tāwhiao, and his supporters were driven out in 1863 by the British, who were at that time invading south from Auckland. Thereafter, the leadership of the movement was exiled to other places in the North Island for some decades.

The modern Tūrangawaewae marae owes its existence to Te Puea Hērangi, a remarkable leader who came from the family of the first Māori king, Potatau.

In the days of Te Puea's youth the Māori King was named Mahuta. Mahuta was the third Māori King. Te Puea persuaded everyone in the court to move back to Ngāruawāhia, and specifically to the new marae, or complex, they called Tūrangawaewae.

Most New Zealand hot springs are heated by volcanic heat, and this usually brings a sulfur smell. But 24 kilometres west of Ngāruawāhia there are the Waingaro Hot Springs: which are unusual for New Zealand because they don't smell of sulfur.

We're not talking about a scooped-out hole in the sand here: Waingaro Hot Springs is a big facility, complete with a hydroslide and a hotel.

On the main highway north out of Hamilton / Kirikiriroa, you come to Huntly, an old coal mining town and the site of an elegant-looking power station that's run on natural gas these days to try and curb its greenhouse emissions, and the town of Taupiri, under Taupiri Mountain: a sacred burial site for high-ranking Māori since the 1600s.

***Taupiri and Taupiri Mountain** (Waikato District Council)*

Further north, on the way back to Auckland, you come to another important battlefield at Rangiriri, where, in November 1863, no less than eight successive assaults by 1,400 British troops failed to capture a massive fort, which was only taken in the end by deception. If this hadn't happened, the invasion of the Waikato might have failed.

The repulse of the Royal Navy storming party, Rangiriri Pā. (20th November 1863). 1863 sketch by Charles Heaphy, from 'The New Zealand Wars', vol. I, by James Cowan. 1922, p. 331. Public domain image via Wikimedia Commons.

The fort was known by both sides as the Rangiriri Pā, the word pā originally meaning a fortified village or stockade, though by the 1860s the word had come to be applied to colossal fortifications that looked like something out of the American

Civil War: the victory of the British by no means assured, though they did win in the end.

There's a cafe with assorted battlefield memorabilia at Rangiriri. The battlefield has lately been restored, after having had a road built through it at one time. For more on all this you may wish to check out the blog post linked at the end of this chapter.

Travelling north past Rangiriri you get to Meremere. The foundations of the fort from which the *Pioneer* was fired upon still exist there. Te Araroa, the long pathway by which you can bike or hike the length of New Zealand, goes right past.

The turrets of the *Pioneer* have been preserved along the lower Waikato, at Mercer and also at Ngāruawāhia. The hull of another of the old-time river monitors, the *Rangiriri,* has also been preserved in Hamilton / Kirikiriroa.

Your last historical turnoff before Auckland would be to Pukekohe East, once more covered in the following blog post.

Blog post with more images:

a-maverick.com/blog/carrying-on-down-the-waikato-part-two

TOUR 4: The Volcanic Desert, the Thermal Region and Lake Waikaremoana

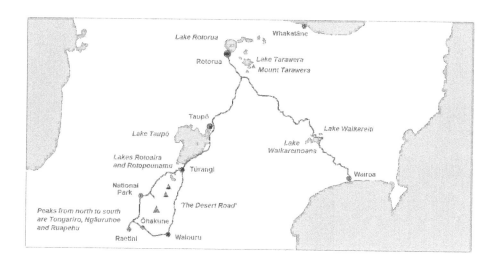

CHAPTER TWENTY-ONE

Mount Ruapehu: You can make it

IN THE CENTRE of the North Island, the sprawling Tongariro National Park area is hard to miss with its three volcanic peaks of Ruapehu, Tongariro and Ngāuruhoe jutting out of the bare high plains of the Central North Island, southwest of Lake Taupō.

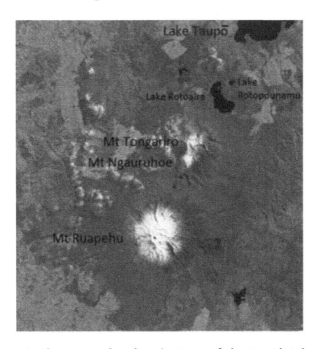

Key Features in the Central Volcanic Area of the North Island. Source: Public domain image from NASA Global Wind, accessed from the webpage commons.wikimedia.org/wiki/File:Tongariro_NP_satellite.jpg in February 2017. Text added for this book.

Mount Ruapehu has two skifields, at Tūroa and Whakapapa, and is very popular with skiers from Auckland. I've also done three snowcraft and climbing courses on Mount Ruapehu and climbed to the top.

Beginning to get icicles in my hair

Hut buried by snow

The name Ruapehu means 'exploding hole', a testament to the fact that the volcano is occasionally active, and perpetually steaming.

I also did a stint as a volunteer DOC warden at the Whakapapaiti Hut for a week over Christmas one year. This hut is part of the Round-the-Mountain Track, a more remote alternative to the popular Northern Circuit. The Round-the-Mountain Track takes four to six days to complete and covers a loop of the mountain of just over 66 kilometres.

I have done the full track and also just the slightly more than ten kilometre walk between Whakapapaiti Hut and the next hut at Mangaturuturu, where there are beautiful views across to Mount Taranaki.

On another topic, DOC has made a huge effort to bring blue ducks, or whio, back by breeding them in sheltered concrete areas with netting over the top to keep them protected. Whio are 'torrent ducks' that don't live in ponds and slow rivers like most sorts of duck, but only in fast mountain streams. There are successful breeding programmes in the South Island as well, but I was blown away by the blue duck programme I saw at Mount Ruapehu. They breed around a hundred of these birds every year – a substantial number that must be one of the biggest breeding programmes in the country.

Keep abreast of the snow reports and skifield cams on **mtruapehu.com**. There's also a sightseeing gondola called the Sky Waka that runs between the Whakapapa skifield and a café on top of a cliff at Knoll Ridge (2020 metres) with great views both up and down the mountain, which you can book on the same website.

Blog post with more images:

a-maverick.com/blog/mount-ruapehu-you-can-make-it

CHAPTER TWENTY-TWO

Mt Tongariro and the Tongariro Crossing: a gem

U NLIKE the sheer peaks of Mount Ruapehu and nearby Mount Ngāuruhoe, Mount Tongariro has a series of spread-out slopes and craters and can be ascended as the one-day Alpine crossing, or as part of the longer three to four day Tongariro Northern Circuit, which is one of New Zealand's Great Walks.

(By the way, it is strongly, officially, recommended that anyone who is not a serious mountaineer should *not* attempt the Tongariro crossing, or circuit, in the more wintery months between early May and late October. The same goes for all New Zealand's Great Walks. They are only 'walks' in season.)

DOC has a good page on the Tongariro Northern Circuit and other walks, with two brochures, one on the Northern Circuit and one on other walks. I've reproduced the key map from the Tongariro Northern Circuit brochure below, up to date as of the time of writing. Make sure to download the latest if you are going there, and get a better map for actual navigation as the DOC one is information only.

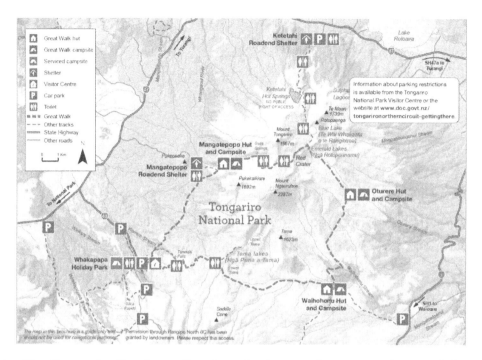

The Tongariro Northern Circuit and other tracks. *Note at bottom left in the original includes a warning that this is not to be used as a navigational map, that it is for information only. From* Tongariro Northern Circuit *(PDF), Wellington, Department of Conservation, September 2019.*

The wider Tongariro area, including Mounts Ngāuruhoe and Ruapehu, was the first national park to be created in New Zealand when the powerful Ngāti Tūwharetoa iwi, or tribe, aligned their fortunes with the Crown and began to open up their lands for tourism in 1887. It is now one of a limited number of World Heritage Sites of joint natural and cultural significance.

When I first tramped Tongariro, I did the full Northern Circuit, and it was beautiful. From Whakapapa Village, we tramped eight and a half kilometres across the plains underneath the famous Mount Ngāuruhoe, which some film buffs might recognise as Mount Doom from the *Lord of the Rings* trilogy. We stopped at Mangatepopo Hut at the entrance of the Tongariro Alpine Crossing, which we joined the following day, and hiked through to Oturere Hut – a five-hour walk of almost thirteen kilometres – passing the beautiful Emerald and Blue Lakes (the Blue Lake is also sacred or tapu to Māori, and needs to be treated similarly to a mountain peak).

The Emerald Lakes

From Oturere it was a further three-hour walk to Waihohonu Hut, before the final stretch — a hike of just over fourteen kilometres through the Tama Saddle between Mt Ngāuruhoe and Mt Ruapehu — to return to our starting point at Whakapapa Village.

I thought I'd make the most of my time in the national park and headed over to tramp the start of the one-day Tongariro Alpine Crossing.

We tramped up over the central crater of Tongariro, where the snow was quite deep. I soon learnt that tramping with crampons on becomes easier if you follow in the footsteps of the person in front of you. The walk had steep drops, and we had to self-arrest with our ice-axes several times to stop ourselves falling down them, so I was thankful we'd learnt how to do it properly on the snowcraft course.

Despite the cold, the tramp to Ketatahi Hut was well worth it, with magnificent views of Lake Rotoaira, Mount Pihanga and even the distant Lake Taupō. The hut is now a museum and shelter, as the greater part of it was destroyed in 2012 when the mountain erupted. I was there at the time, as I was planning to climb Mount Tongariro when a crater called Te Maari blew.

All the volcanic mountains in the Tongariro National Park are still active. So, in addition to the usual hazards you have when tramping in mountainous areas, there's also the added risk of volcanic activity. As such, DOC recommends that all trampers intending to trek the crossing should check in on the current volcanic alert level of the mountains at one of their offices, or online, before setting out.

I love the grasses and the smell on Tongariro when you first start out, and don't mind the weather.

Blog post with more images:

a-maverick.com/blog/mount-tongariro-crossing-a-gem

CHAPTER TWENTY-THREE

Lakes Rotoaira and Rotopounamu

ALSO well worth a visit are Lakes Rotoaira and Rotopounamu, two beautiful lakes which lie halfway between the volcanoes of Tongariro National Park and Lake Taupō.

Both lakes are bordered by native bush and closely overlooked by the bald-topped Mount Pihanga, visible at centre-right in the aerial photograph below.

Aerial image showing locations of Lake Rotoaira and the smaller Lake Rotopounamu near the red highway shield marked '47'. Source: Google Earth, imagery ©2017 DigitalGlobe, Waikato District Council, Horizons Regional Consortium, Map Data ©2017 Google.

A view of Lake Rotoaira from Mount Tongariro

Lake Rotoaira was raised in the 1970s for the purposes of the Tongariro Power Scheme. It is privately owned and for that reason, you need a permit to go boating or fishing.

But the smaller of the two lakes, Lake Rotopounamu, is quite unmodified, public, and surrounded by bush. A walking track, off State Highway 47, goes all the way around Lake Rotopounamu.

Blog post with more images:

a-maverick.com/blog/lakes-rotoaira-and-rotopounamu-between-volcanoes-taupo

CHAPTER TWENTY-FOUR

Taupō to Rotorua: A Māori Yellowstone and a Jurassic Forest

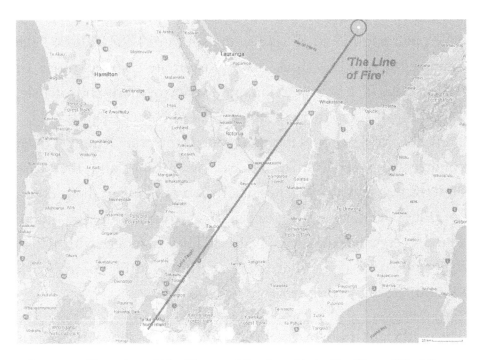

Rotorua, Taupō and the Thermal Region. *Note the 'line of fire' from Whakaari / White Island (circled) through to the large volcanoes of the central North Island via the Rotorua and Taupō districts. Background map data ©2020 Google.*

NO ACCOUNT of New Zealand would be complete without a description of the Rotorua thermal region and

Lake Taupō. Rotorua was one of New Zealand's original tourist destinations both for cultural and spa-town reasons, and is well worth visiting for a more traditional tourism experience. The same is true of Taupō, the inland great lake at the centre of the North Island, which is popular with yachties and trout-fishers.

In fact, the whole area around Lake Taupō is very popular for fishing. Many bodies of water in this area including the Tongariro River, and another small lake to the south of Lake Taupō, Lake Otamangakau, were stocked with trout in colonial times or thereabouts. The town of Tūrangi at the southern end of Lake Taupō is called the trout fishing capital of New Zealand.

At the Tongariro National Trout Centre in Tūrangi, trout congregate under a small bridge for feeding, and there are underwater viewing windows where you can look at them eye to eye. Plus, a café where you can dine on trout. Trout aren't to be found everywhere in New Zealand. They compete with native fish, and in certain other areas of the country no trout (or salmon) are allowed to exist these days.

The official tourism website for the Taupō region is **lovetaupo.com**.

Lakes Rotorua and Taupō both lie on a geological 'line of fire' that runs from Whakaari / White Island through to Tongariro National Park. The whole Rotorua region is a caldera similar to Yellowstone National Park in the USA, and Taupō is of similarly explosive origin, though there are fewer boiling springs in the immediate vicinity as compared to Rotorua.

Mount Tarawera, one of the four main points of interest in the region, erupted in a devastating cataclysm in 1886, during which the earth quite simply burst open, forming a chasm on the top of Mount Tarawera.

The author in the crater of Mount Tarawera

There is more to the region than geology. As I've just suggested, Māori culture is strong in the region (I will come back to that). Also, there are tramping and biking trails and, curiously enough, at Whakarewarewa, a forest of Californian coastal redwoods.–. *sequoia sempervirens*.–. planted as part of an experimental logging scheme in 1901 and never harvested.

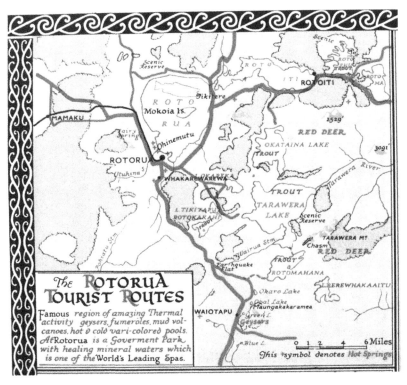

Map of the Rotorua area dated 1946, a detail from a larger 'Tourist Map of New Zealand' drawn for the NZ Government Tourist Board, on display at the Auckland Public Library in April 2018. The "chasm" at the top of Mount Tarawera is much longer than shown. Crown Copyright reserved.

The Real Jurassic Park

As in California, the redwoods are becoming sacred now and nobody would dream of chopping them down anymore. The tall trees have become part of the local scenery and populate of the landscape of many Kiwis' childhood holiday memories too.

From a genus (*sequoia*) which was widespread in the age of the dinosaurs, but with their natural range now confined to California, the redwoods now growing at Whakarewarewa provide shade for an understory of equally ancient tree ferns: a type of plant which was also common in the dinosaur age, but which later died out in North America. Tree ferns did, however, survive in New Zealand.

At Whakarewarewa, the redwoods and the tree ferns dwell together to re-create an ecosystem not seen since the age of the dinosaurs. The same pairing of North American redwoods and giant tree ferns has sprung up in other locations where redwoods have been introduced, such as Lucys Gully in Taranaki. But Whakarewarewa is perhaps the best place to see it, for you can see the combination of ferns and redwoods from the trails or from above, on the 23 suspension bridges of Whakarewarewa's Redwoods Treewalk.

The Thin Crust of Rotorua

The 1886 eruption of Mount Tarawera destroyed the Pink and White Terraces: natural wonders that were just starting to become known to the wealthy-tourist trade.

Two Victorian paintings by Charles Blomfield capture the beauty of the White Terrace and the horror of the subsequent eruption of Mount Tarawera, in which the earth quite literally burst open. The upper painting has accession number 1894/4 at the Auckland City Art Gallery (gift of Sir Henry Brett, 1894) and the lower painting is item C-033–022, National Library of New Zealand.

The pink and white terraces were made from a stalactite-like mineral called travertine, deposited by warm springs as they trickled down the hillside.

Mid-twentieth century tourism poster advertising the buried village of Te Wairoa, on the shores of Lake Tarawera. Mount Tarawera is visible in the background.

About a hundred to a hundred and fifty people were killed when Mt Tarawera erupted in 1886, including a tohunga (Māori shaman), who was said to have predicted the eruption. He was dug out alive from under the ash at the village of Te Wairoa, often simply referred to these days as the buried village, but succumbed a little later.

Clobbered by Cyclones, too

When I was there, the area got hammered by ex-tropical Cyclone Hola, a Fijian name. The day before the cyclone, I got some good photos of the freaky clouds that came before it. This part of New Zealand often gets the tail end of tropical cyclones, something that adds to its generally precarious nature and the feeling that nature is in command.

The sky just before Cyclone Hola hit

The Guardians of the Volcano

Tours to the top of Mount Tarawera are operated, these days, by a Māori agency called Kaitiaki Adventures.

Kaitiaki means 'guardian' or 'guardians', and the name refers to the fact that earlier, unregulated tourism had left the mountain covered in rubbish. At one time, a truck was hired, and filled, with junk picked up from the mountain. So, these days, the tourist has to go on a tour organised by Kaitiaki Adventures.

Another important example of Māori tourism operation in the vicinity of Rotorua and Tarawera is the village at Whakarewarewa, the 'living Māori village' which has been occupied since before the coming of Europeans to the area, and where tourists can sample the delights of food cooked the old-fashioned way in naturally boiling pools.

Return to Rotorua

I was able to stay on a campsite at the Rotorua Thermal Park for only NZ $20 a night (they also have cabins), taking advantage of the hot pools, which have a range of temperatures. I had Māori massage which was offered in two forms, the relaxing Mirimiri and the deeper and harder Romiromi technique. The Hawai'ians have a form of traditional massage called Lomilomi, so I imagine these techniques have been around for a long time. The woman giving me the massage said that she had to concentrate and breathe white light into my soul and the areas of the body that are sore. Her grandmother was a fully-fledged Māori healer, she told me.

Like much of New Zealand, Rotorua feels a bit more sophisticated than it used to be. Its downtown has been greatly beautified, and I went to a Tunisian restaurant, something that is obviously par for the course these days.

Here is the sign advertising Māori massage where I went, plus a photo of a Māori Jesus over Lake Rotorua at St Faith's Church, Ohinemutu, wearing a similar cloak to the one worn by NZ Prime Minister Jacinda Ardern when she went to see the Queen recently. The Māori Jesus photograph is by 'Cherub51', CC-BY-SA 3.0 via Wikimedia Commons.

The Māori village, and thermal scenes, at Whakarewarewa

Downtown Rotorua

Blog post with more images:

a-maverick.com/blog/maori-yellowstone-jurassic-forest

CHAPTER TWENTY-FIVE

Waikaremoana: Also Steeped in Māoritanga

AS A CHILD I gained a strong connection to Lake Waikaremoana, the lake of rippling waters, which is located in the Māori stewardship area of Te Urewera (formerly Te Urewera National Park). Since Waikaremoana is only a few hours north of Hastings, my family used to camp out at the lake every Christmas holiday from when I was six years old until I was about sixteen. I tramped the area extensively in 1995 and 1998 and redid it in 2008 and in 2012 – I always seem to keep coming back there.

The area is home to the Ngāi Tūhoe iwi, and even as a young child I recognised their strong presence in the area. I remember that when we would drive into Murupara we would always being amazed at how everyone working in the shop spoke Māori.

Here's the DOC information page for Lake Waikaremoana:
doc.govt.nz/parks-and-recreation/places-to-go/east-coast/places/te-urewera/things-to-do/tracks/lake-waikaremoana-great-walk/

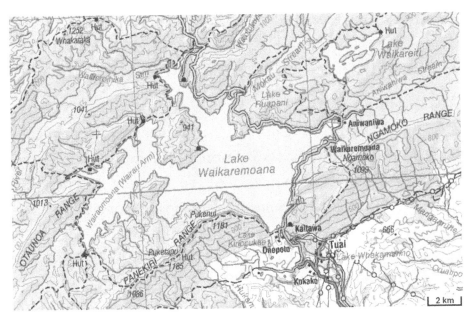

Lakes Waikaremoana and Waikareiti with nearby tramping tracks.
Map data by LINZ via <u>NZ Topo Map</u>, 2020.

The remote Te Urewera area has been home to Ngāi Tūhoe, meaning the Tūhoe people or tribe, for centuries; and it was they who named the lake 'Waikaremoana', which means 'sea of the rippling waters'. Tūhoe did not sign the Treaty of Waitangi and have a strong history of seeking independence from the British Crown.

A short hike from the visitor centre takes you to the nearby Lake Waikareiti, meaning the little rippling waters. It's a great place to for kayaking, and if you kayak out to Rāhui Island and climb the metal ladder, you can see the beautiful Lake Tamaiti o

Waikaremoana, or little child of the rippling waters – a lake within a lake!

My friends and I had stopped by Tamaiti o Waikaremoana to camp out, and another tramper on the island came up to me and gave me some trout so I gave him a bag of marshmallows and some biscuits in return. He told me that he was fishing and hunting, and was planning to take some of the extra venison he'd caught to another island on the lake where local Māori were camping. He said that the Tūhoe had a tradition that if they turn up three weeks before Christmas and name their campground by staking their rights to Māori land, they can stay there for free.

I tramped the Waikaremoana Track, which leads around the lake. One of the few New Zealand Great Walks in the North Island, the track cuts its way through the thick bush surrounding the lake.

The Lake Waikaremoana track reminded me of Mount Pirongia in the Waikato area, as they both have cabbage trees and Dicksonia ferns. These beautiful native trees can be seen all over New Zealand in areas ranging from home gardens to wild bush. The cabbage tree tends to prefer wide open spaces such as farms where it gets full sunlight. The area around Lake Waikaremoana is also home to many other native New Zealand plants and birds.

We took the roughly nine-kilometre route from Onepoto to Panekire Hut, which takes about five hours according to DOC and is the only major uphill part of the walk. However, the views from the top of Panekire make it worth it – on a good day you can see right out to Wairoa and Gisborne.

Why I keep coming back to Lake Waikaremoana *(lake views are from Panekire Bluff)*

Korokoro Falls

The next day we continued our tramp, walking mostly downhill in the seven-and-a-half kilometre stretch from Panekire Hut to Waiopaoa Hut, which takes about three to four hours. This section of the tramp is filled with beech, podocarp and kāmahi trees, and it was just beautiful. From Waiopaoa Hut we carried on to Marauiti Hut for the second-longest stretch of walking through just over twelve kilometres of forest alongside the lake. This took us a little over five hours to complete, and along the way we passed some private baches owned by some renowned Hawkes Bay families, where we stopped and had lunch.

We had an uneventful stay at Marauiti Hut before the final stretch to Hopuruahine Landing, which, at 17 km, is easily the longest section of the Waikaremoana Track. Still, it was a lovely, moderate walk by the lakeside that only took us about half a day to complete. When we finally arrived at the landing, we decided to finish our tramp with a swim, which was very refreshing after the long day.

Blog post with more images:

a-maverick.com/blog/waikaremoana-also-steeped-in-maoritanga

TOUR 5: Hawkes Bay and the Wairarapa

CHAPTER TWENTY-SIX

From Te Kurī to Te Mata: What you will see as you leave Gisborne for Hawkes Bay

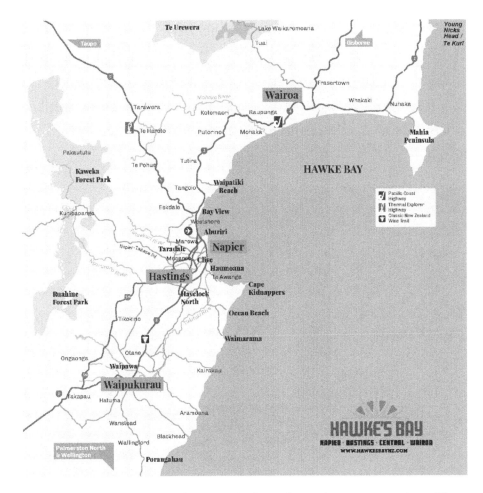

Map reproduced with the permission of Hawkes Bay Tourism. The words 'Young Nicks Head / Te Kurī' added for this book, at top right.

HEADING SOUTH from Gisborne you come to a headland called Young Nicks Head or Te Kurī ('the dog'), short for Te Kurī-a-Pāoa, 'Pāoa's dog', after the legendary captain of the ancestral *Horouta* voyaging-canoe, also known as Pāwa.

The name Young Nicks Head was bestowed by Captain Cook in honour of the cabin boy, Nicholas Young, who was the first of Cook's crew to catch sight of New Zealand, at this spot.

There's a big wetland just to the Head's north called the Wherowhero Lagoon and a smaller, award-winning wetland called the Orongo Wetland to its south, leading down to Orongo Beach.

It's a surprisingly long way from Gisborne to the next conurbation to the south, the twin cities of Napier and Hastings. More than 200 kilometres.

On the way to Māhia you go past the Morere Hot Springs and Scenic Reserve.

The pools were long known to local Māori before being 'discovered' by Europeans, who turned them into a government resort and in so doing, saved the now-rare Nīkau palm forest that surrounded them from being logged and turned into farmland.

I also visited the nearby Mangaone Caves Scenic Reserve, mostly notable for its rugged terrain.

Māhia

At the Māhia Peninsula, the Rocket Lab launch site is located at its southern tip. It would be a good idea for a regional holiday if you timed a visit to see a rocket go off, with other activities before and after. The launch dates and times are announced on the Internet on various sites, including Rocket Lab's Facebook page.

One thing you could do to while away the time would be to freedom-camp at Opoutama, or Blue Bay, on the west side of the narrow neck of land that joins the peninsula to the mainland. And enjoy the bay and Mahanga Beach on the east side of the narrow neck of land, and climb Mokotahi Lookout, head down Kinikini Road to the Māhia Scenic Reserve and do the Māhia Peninsula Track.

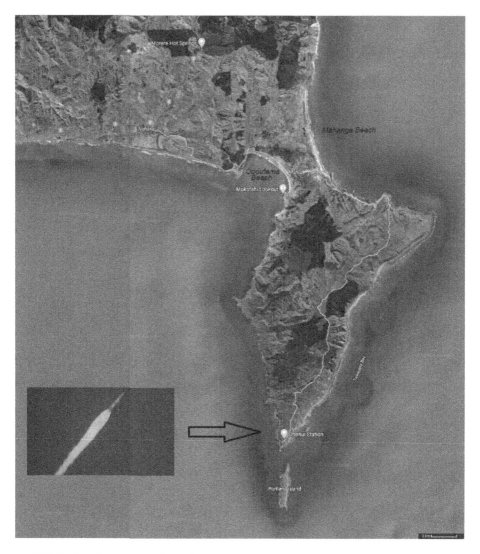

Māhia Peninsula and Environs. *Names of Opoutama and Mahanga Beaches plus NASA image of Saturn V (Apollo) rocket added for this book. Background imagery ©2020 Terrametrics, background map data ©2020 Google.*

I think a rocket launch would cap that off very nicely!

From Māhia, I drove on to Wairoa on the much larger <u>Hawke Bay</u>. The region that has Hawke Bay for its seafront is known as Hawkes Bay with an s, and no apostrophe strictly speaking either.

So, Wairoa is on Hawke Bay but in Hawkes Bay. Which seems a little odd: but there you are.

Check out the website of Hawkes Bay Tourism, on **hawkesbaynz.com**.

Wairoa has an attractive riverside embankment called Marine Parade even though it's on a river. There are no buildings on the river side, only a park, and many fine old buildings face the river from across the street.

The town has a long history of Māori occupation and many historic sites, and it also sits at the heart of a number of tracks and scenic reserves in the surrounding country.

Napier

The next big town or city is Napier, a town that has literally risen out of the sea. Napier was founded on an island known to Māori as Mataruahou and to the colonists as Scinde Island.

The modern town has a really classy, Riviera-like quality enhanced by a tree-lined Marine Parade of its own, actually marine this time, as well as a lot of crisp-looking 1930s architecture.

In the old days many Māori lived on Mataruahou, where at one location a stream descends down a cleft in a local cliff.

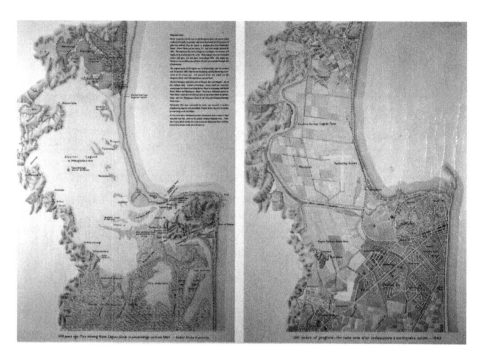

'Napier – 100 Years of Progress' Map (1965). Hawkes Bay Digital Archives Trust, CC-BY-NC 4.0.

In a local legend a mermaid named Pania, married to a human husband named Karitoki, could not continue to return to the sea if she ate cooked food on land. So, one night, Karitoki put cooked food in her mouth as she was sleeping in the hope that she would swallow it and thus stay with him all day. But just at that moment Pania was awakened by the warning cry of an owl and ran to the sea in horror, whereupon the sea-people dragged her down and she was never seen by Karitoki again.

A statue of Pania, generally known as 'Pania of the Reef', was unveiled in 1954. Here's a photo taken in 1967 for New Zealand's National Publicity Studios by Gregor Riethmaier.

'"Pania of the Reef" on the Marine Parade, Napier'. Archives New Zealand AAQT 6539 W3537 68 A80964, CC-BY-SA 2.0 via Wikimedia Commons.

And here's me beside it!

I popped into the local museum and saw a carved panel called a poupou, advertised as the last remaining in the region from a failed 1870s project to build a great, new, Māori meeting-house to be called Heretaunga III, which would have been erected at Pākōwhai, just outside Hastings.

The project was initiated by Karaitiana Takamoana, Member of the House of Representatives for Eastern Māori in the 1870s.

Like the whole of New Zealand and many parts of the North Island in particular, Napier has a strong Māori heritage. But the area was soon lost to European colonists.

The Great Earthquake

On the third of February 1931 there was a massive earthquake, followed by fires. The whole region was affected, though it is called the Napier Earthquake because the damage was worst in Napier.

And so, the whole downtown was rebuilt in reinforced concrete as a Depression-era public works project, in record time.—. about two years.—. and in a style the locals call Art Deco, though that's disputed by the purists.

Downtown Napier after the 1931 Earthquake: *this view includes the Anglican Cathedral, which was entirely rebuilt in reinforced concrete (Napier City Council)*

An organisation called the Art Deco Trust operates out of one of the downtown buildings, running bus tours.

Modernism and the idea of rebuilding everything from scratch isn't confined to the central city. There's a whole suburb of early-modern-architecture houses called Marewa, which is also surrounded by a belt of parkland with walking paths along it.

Napier's Marine Parade, another product of the rebuilding years of the 1930s, fronts onto Napier Beach. Which unfortunately isn't very good.

But Ahuriri Beach, adjacent to Spriggs Park on the northern side of Mataruahou, is much better. So is the beach on the former sandspit that used to guard the old lagoon to the west, the beach known as Westshore Beach, which only has the disadvantage of not being so close to town.

It was really the 1931 earthquake that sealed the demise of the Napier lagoons, by raising the land a couple of metres.

While I was in Napier, I also saw an information panel showing some of the tramping, biking and wine trails of southern Hawkes Bay. These include visits to sites of Māori heritage such as a remarkably preserved old-time hilltop pā at Otatara, accessible via the Otatara Pā Loop Trail.

You can browse the trails, download a trail map and get the app from **hbtrails.nz**.

Waitangi Regional Park

A little way south, I came to a place called Waitangi Regional Park where the Tutaekuri River, the Ngaruroro River and the Clive River all come together and flow out to the sea through a common mouth, with the Tukituki River a little further along down the coast.

The Waitangi ('weeping waters') Regional Park has a circle of carved poles erected just in the last couple of years, called Ātea a Rangi or heavenly court, which honours the rising of Matariki and also symbolises various aspects of Polynesian navigation.

There is a good account of Polynesian voyaging techniques by Rāwiri Taonui, 'Canoe Navigation', on *Te Ara,* the online encyclopaedia of New Zealand. The link is **teara.govt.nz/en/canoe-navigation**.

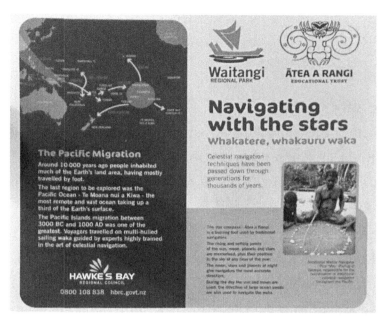

From a sign information board that I saw at the Waitangi Regional Park, south of Napier

Hastings and Havelock

After Napier, I popped into Hastings, where I grew up. Somewhat inland, Hastings has long been considered to be a bit more working-class than Napier. It was smashed up in the 1931 earthquake as well, if not quite so drastically, and also got some Art Deco buildings to replace the ones destroyed.

Growing up in Hastings gave me a very outdoor lifestyle. I probably played about eight sports at secondary school and was always outside and active.

My favourite beaches were Ocean Beach and Waimarama, both within half an hour's drive of Hastings, or so. They have golden sand and I remember doing a lot of boogie boarding. There are other well-known surfing beaches like Te Awana, Waipatiki Beach and Haumoana but they are more stony. And a lot of wineries.

Havelock North is a nice town as well, just south of Hastings. There's a good account of things that you can do in and around Havelock North on the Hawkes Bay Tourism website, as also for other parts of Hawkes Bay. There are several wineries nearby, the town itself is quite picturesque with streets radiating out from the centre and the Karituwhenua Stream walkway in the suburbs, Plus it's also on the way to Te Mata Peak, which I'm going to talk about in the last section of this chapter.

You can download a Havelock North parks and trails map from the website **havelocknorthnz.com**.

Te Mata

Finally, another place you have to visit is Te Mata Peak (meaning 'the face').

Te Mata Peak

Te Mata Peak is like an immense wave in the land, with exposed limestone tops as the equivalent of the wave's white foam. You can go all the way to the top and look out.

Blog post with more images:

a-maverick.com/blog/from-te-kuri-to-te-mata-what-you-will-see-as-you-leave-gisborne-for-hawkes-bay

Lands east of the Ruahine Forest Park are in Central Hawkes Bay, lands east of the Tararua Forest Park are in the Wairarapa: The Manawatū Gorge / Te Āpiti divides the Ruahine and Tararua Ranges. Background map data ©2020 Google. Names of Hawke Bay, Cape Kidnappers / Te Kauwae-a-Māui, Manawatū Gorge / Te Āpiti, Central Hawkes Bay, The Wairarapa, Lake Wairarapa, Maungaraki, Putangirua Pinnacles and Ngawi have been added for this book. Haurangi Forest Park is an old name, the correct name is now Aorangi.

CHAPTER TWENTY-SEVEN

East of the Ranges: Central Hawkes Bay and the Wairarapa

ANOTHER place we used to visit when I was a kid in Hastings was Cape Kidnappers/Te Kauwae-a-Māui ('the jawbone of Māui'), an amazing headland that sticks out a long way into the Pacific at the southern end of Hawke Bay, a bit like Young Nicks Head / Te Kurī only bigger. The Cape has a gannet colony at its tip.

Cape Kidnappers / Te Kauwae-a-Māui from a point near its tip. Photograph by Nicolas Aub, 10 January 2016, CC-BY-2.0 via Wikimedia Commons.

253

'Uncaptioned photograph of bird colony, possibly gannets at Cape Kidnappers Archives New Zealand Reference: AEFZ 22625 W5727 2598 /3103/0209', undated image, CC-BY-2.0 via Wikimedia Commons. For "possible" read almost certainly. That's certainly what the colony is like.

We would pile into informal trailers and the 4WD Gannet Safari bus that drove along the beach all the way past the huge cliffs that faced north, all the way out to the tip where the gannets wheeled and dived and thronged in huge numbers.

These days, there's a road to the tip of the headland and nobody drives along the beach to get to the gannet colony anymore, though you can still walk it at low tide if you're brave enough, as it's considered too dangerous due to the fact that the cliffs keep falling down.

This July, I headed south from Hastings into the area known as Central Hawkes Bay, even though it's actually to the south of the Bay.

There are actually seventeen Heritage Trails in Hawkes Bay, most of them in the southern part of Hawkes Bay.

I drove south past Te Aute, the famous Māori college where the sons of chiefs and future Māori Members of Parliament were educated a hundred years ago, Ōtāne, Waipukurau where they filmed the new movie about an over-zealous cop called *This Town* .—. Hawkes Bay's trying to attract more interest from filmmakers via an organisation called the Eastern Screen Alliance.—. and on into 'Central'.

I carried on down toward the Manawatū Gorge, known as Te Āpiti ('the gorge') in Māori. Te Āpiti is also the name of a local website describing the gorge's history and things to do.

The Manawatū Gorge / Te Āpiti looking west from the Te Āpiti -
Manawatū Gorge Track, *showing State Highway 3 (now closed by*
rockfalls) on the left and the Palmerston North-to-Gisborne railway line
on the right. Public domain image (24 May 2008) by 'SmokeySteve',
via Wikimedia Commons.

In Te Āpiti, which I'll also call the Gorge, the Manawatū River rises on the east and flows west through a crack in the ranges, called the Ruahine Range to the north and the Tararua Range to the south. The river is older than the mountains and has stubbornly cut downwards even as the mountains have risen.

Here, too, the cliffs keep falling down. The government is building a new main highway to the north of the Gorge, after having given up on 150 years of keeping the old route free of rockfalls.

There are massive windfarms to the north and south of the Gorge, where the wind funnels through between the two ranges. The total capacity of these wind farms is 300.25 megawatts, which is getting up there by wind power standards.

New Zealand has been described as the 'Saudi Arabia of wind', the resource so abundant and continual that the wind farms flanking the Gorge have been built without subsidies.

Before the turnoff to the Gorge, I passed the Scandinavian settlement of Norsewood and then another, larger one called Dannevirke. The name Dannevirke means 'earthwork of the Danes' and only has one 'n' in the original Danish: an additional 'n' was added so that British neighbours would pronounce it correctly.

In 1987, the town was visited by Queen Margarethe II of Denmark.

Carrying on through Woodville and Pahiatua, not turning into the Gorge but carrying on south, I came to the town of Mangatainoka, famous for its historic Tui Brewery.

Pūkaha National Wildlife Centre (Mount Bruce)

Eventually, I came to the Pūkaha National Wildlife Centre, just before a pass on the edge of the Tararua Range called Mount Bruce.

These days they've got a white kiwi: a bashful little creature which features prominently on the Pūkaha website. It's certainly easier to see in the dim light of the kiwi-house than the usual brown, grey or spotted ones!

The reserve was greatly expanded by the gift of Rangitāne land in 2016 and encompasses a whole lot of remnant native forest from what used to be called the 'Seventy Mile Bush'.

There's also the historic Kaiparoro Anzac Memorial Bridge in this area, accessible by a trail through the forest in a nearby spot called the W. A. Miller Scenic Reserve. Anzac is short for Australia and New Zealand Army Corps. The 25th of April is called Anzac Day in New Zealand and is celebrated as a public holiday.

The Glistening Waters and 'Where the Sky Runs'

Somewhere before Pūkaha, I'd crossed into a region called the Wairarapa, though it's not much different to Central Hawkes Bay: just further south. The Wairarapa continues the landscape that's east of the Tararua Range all the way to Cape Palliser, the southernmost tip of the North Island.

> Destination Wairarapa is the official travel resource for the Wairarapa: **wairarapanz.com**.

The name Wairarapa means 'glistening waters' and probably refers to what's now called Lake Wairarapa, a large but shallow lake near the southern end of the region.

The Tararua Range forms a boundary between local Māori iwi, as many natural features do. In the 1820s a chief named Te Whiwhi negotiated an agreement between Ngāti Toa, who had lately conquered lands to the west of the Tararua Range, that they would not cross the range and make war on the Ngāti Kahungunu in the east, nor vice versa.

Masterton is named after Joseph Masters, a nineteenth-century land reformer and founder of the town. To this day, some of the land in and around Masterton is held in common by all the citizens. Utopian social experiments of that sort were quite common in colonial New Zealand.

On the one hand there is the question of lands unjustly taken from Māori and the issue of the taking of too much land. The colonial experience showed both tendencies.

From Masterton, I went north-east to Castlepoint, the best beach-holiday destination on the Wairarapa coast.

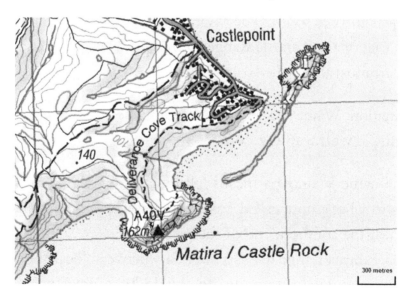

Castlepoint / Rangiwhakaoma. *Map data by LINZ via NZ Topo Map,*
2020.

Castlepoint is another Captain Cook name. The location is known in Māori as Rangiwhakaoma, 'where the sky runs', because it's rather windy and has lots of rapidly scudding cloud. Not ideal for a beach destination I know, but it's a beach of the bracing kind, at least.

In any case, the main attraction is not the beach or the sun but rather the incredible rock formations that inspired Cook to give it that name, in the form of a rock called Matira / Castle Rock and an offshore reef that impounds an ever-changing system of sandy lagoons.

It's a high-energy sort of a place.

A selfie in the wind!

The Castlepoint Lighthouse, which is accessible to walkers via a track

A photo of the Castlepoint Lighthouse on top of these rocks is on the landing page of the New Zealand Department of Conservation's *Wairarapa: Places to Go* guide.

There's a track to a place called Deliverance Cove, a name that references the 1843 shipwreck of several missionaries based up the coast at Ahuriri, the locality where the town of Napier would later be founded. (They survived, whence the name.)

And lots of sea-caves too, plus a town that sells ice-creams. In short, the perfect place for a family holiday.

You can get to Castlepoint by air, as there is an airstrip west of the township. Otherwise, it's a drive from Masterton. You can't get to it by just driving down the coast. One of the peculiarities of the Wairarapa is that the coast is often inaccessible by land, with sheep-stations extending to the high tide mark.

At the Pāpāwai Marae near Greytown I saw a monument to Ngāti Kahungunu leader, runholder and newspaper proprietor Hamuera Tamahau Mahupuku. He was a really interesting person, and I have more about him in the blog post on which this chapter is based.

At the southern end of the region, near Cape Palliser, there's also White Rock Beach, named after a prominent white rock. To get there you have to go inland to a town called Martinborough, which is famous as the hub of a wine-growing district with frequent tastings, and also has the best-stocked i-Site I came across.

Trendy towns and a rail trail

The inland towns of the Wairarapa are all charming, including the smaller ones: Martinborough, Carterton, Greytown and Featherston. The last of these, Featherston, is now a noted international Booktown, a bookish sort of a place with book fairs.

> The Martinborough i-Site was the best one I've visited, with all sorts of maps and resources that I couldn't find elsewhere!

All these towns might have been just farming towns at one time, but these days a lot of Wellingtonians come to the Wairarapa on their days off, and even commute from the Wairarapa via the 8.8 kilometre Rimutaka Tunnel, which was built in the 1950s and is the longest tunnel in New Zealand with scheduled passenger trains.

Today, the route of the old railway over the top is called the Remutaka (with an 'e') Rail Trail, popular with mountain bikers. It's really exposed. One of the spots on the trail is called Siberia, and in the 1880s a train was actually blown off the tracks.

Featherston's also long been the site of military camps and prisoner-of-war camps in both World Wars. During World War One, between thirty and thirty-five thousand troops hiked over the Rimutaka Range from Wellington to camp in Featherston, presumably to help get them fit as they could have caught the train.

Oh yeah, and there's the usual *Lord of the Rings* site.

At the southern tip of the Wairarapa, there are the Cappadocia-like Putangirua Pinnacles and the isolated, south-facing fishing village of Ngāwī. This is one town where things haven't changed much.

Ngāwī. Public domain image by David Blackwell, originally uploaded 29 August 2006, via Wikimedia Commons.

They say that at Ngāwī there are more tractors or bulldozers than people, because there's no jetty and the boats are just dragged in and out of the sea. Ngāwī is at the foot of a really

267

impressive hill which is off to the left of the panorama above, and so it looks a bit like a mini-Cape Town.

Blog post with more images:

a-maverick.com/blog/east-of-the-ranges-central-hawkes-bay-and-the-wairarapa

TOUR 6: Wild, Weird, Windy Wellington

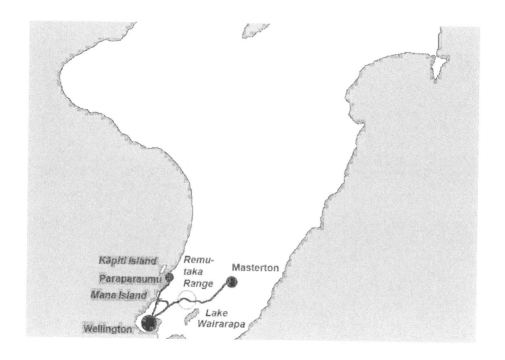

CHAPTER TWENTY-EIGHT

Wild, Weird, Windy Wellington: A capital city at 'the head of Māui's fish'

Wellington and its surroundings. *Imagery ©2020 TerraMetrics, map data ©2020 Google.*

271

O VER THE Remutaka Range from the Wairarapa, you come to Wellington. If the area north of Auckland is the tail of Māui's fish, by the same tradition, Wellington is at the head of the fish, and the city's sizable harbour is deemed to be one of the fish's eyes while the nearby Lake Wairarapa is its other eye.

Woman blown against lamp post, Wellington, 1959. Photographic negatives and prints of the Evening Post and Dominion newspapers. Ref: EP/1959/3756-F. Alexander Turnbull Library, Wellington, New Zealand. /records/22866312.

The roaring forties whip through wherever there is a gap in the mountains. One of these gaps is Te Āpiti, the Manawatū Gorge, the site of all those wind farms.

But the biggest gap is Cook Strait, between the North and South Islands of New Zealand. Where, as it happens, the nation's capital city of Wellington is.

Back in the days when everyone wore hats, Wellington newspapers used to print photos of the local townsfolk hanging onto them.

Wellington's an urban area. But it's crammed in by rugged terrain, and so there a lot of open countryside nearby: often very close nearby. You don't have to stay in a hotel or even in a building. *NZ Pocket Guide* lists fifteen free camping sites in the region. Just make sure that your tent doesn't get blown away!

The city's gorgeous when the sun shines, though. It's like a mini-San Francisco, complete with cable car. The best place to take a picture is at the upper cable-car terminus in the suburb of Kelburn, close to the university. It's a really good spot for selfies or having your picture taken, as well.

'Photo taken from Wellington Botanic Garden lookout in Kelburn, Wellington, New Zealand, looking East. Wellington Cable Car parked over the maintenance pit at Kelburn station. Doors are open. Kelburn Park is undergoing resurfacing in preparation for Cricket season.' Photo by <u>Donaldytong</u>, 2 November 2007, CC-BY-SA 3.0 *via Wikimedia Commons.*

Wellington's actually a hidden gem. There's even a chapter about it in a 1954 book called *Great Cities of the World*. In the 2000s, another book came out called *Why Go to the Riviera: Images of Wellington*. For Wellington's also a city that's been depicted surprisingly often by artists.

And certainly, Wellington does seem like a Mediterranean Riviera, as well as San Francisco. A few years after *Great Cities of the World* came out, the prominent urbanist Nikolaus Pevsner wrote, in a December 1958 *New Zealand Listener* article, that Wellington reminded him very much of the Italian city of Genoa.

Wellington's also the city where New Zealand's most famous writer, Katherine Mansfield, lived.

Katherine Mansfield. *Public domain image via Wikimedia Commons*

Nor is Wellington as enslaved to the car as some other New Zealand cities either. It's very 'urban', perhaps more so than any other city in New Zealand even though Auckland is much bigger. Wellington's café culture remains strong, and there are several boutique cinemas including *Lord of the Rings* director Peter Jackson's new Roxy Cinema.

Wellington is shaped like the letter 'Y' and has very good public transport by New Zealand standards, each leg of the letter served by a public transport spine. The southern leg is served by local buses which run every few minutes, and the two northern legs are served by electric railways. There's talk of extending light rail from the main railway station along the southern leg to Wellington Airport (though so far, it's just talk.)

These days the Wellington waterfront is totally pedestrianised, as you can see already in the following photo, taken in 2008.

Te Papa Tongarewa and the Wellington Free Ambulance Building from Whairepo Lagoon. Image by 'Tākuta', 18 January 2008. CC-BY-SA 2.0 via Wikimedia Commons.

Although downtown Wellington is very modernistic, there is a lot of emphasis on the old-time Māori heritage of the city. There is an official heritage trail that you can follow around Wellington called Te Ara o ngā Tūpuna, 'The Trail of the Ancestors'.

The official tourism website for Wellington is Discover Wellington, **wellingtonnz.com**.

There's also a separate Wellington App.

By tradition the first to see New Zealand was the female figure Kuramārotini, who was either the wife or daughter of the legendary navigator Kupe, and who by some accounts called attention to a white cloud indicating the new land. Kupe and his family are commemorated in a statue which was first unveiled in 1940, to commemorate the 100th anniversary of the signing of the Treaty of Waitangi. These days a bronze copy of the original statue, which was made of plaster and thus not very durable, is down on the Wellington waterfront.

The Kupe Group Statue. *Photo by* Paul Lloyd, *21 December 2009, CC-BY-SA 2.0* **via** *Wikimedia Commons.*

Wellington's been the capital of New Zealand since 1865, so it abounds with the works of officialdom. These include the Old Government Buildings from the 1870s that still dominate much of the downtown. It's actually one building, and one of the largest wooden structures in the world.

The front of the Old Government Buildings, Wellington. *Photo by 'Ballofstring', 11 July 2007, CC-BY-SA 3.0 via Wikimedia Commons.*

Between the monuments and big buildings, little cottages of the kind that were probably inhabited by labourers a hundred years ago still abound.

Old wooden houses on hillsides and clusters of more modern townhouses also contribute to the Wellington look.

Trees that bloom in summer shade the streets.

Thanks in part to all that rugged terrain, the extent of Wellington's parklands really is vast.

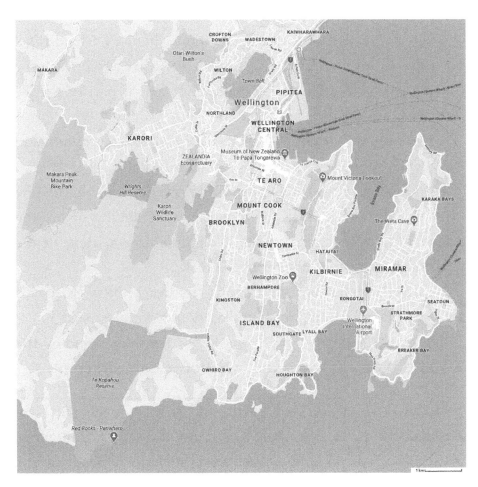

Central and south Wellington and its parklands. *Map data ©2020 Google.*

Wellington's parklands include the western side of Mount Victoria, part of what's called the Town Belt of parklands, which encompasses the downtown area. This was an early experiment in town planning, very similar to what was done in the South Australian capital city of Adelaide.

There's a really handsome Māori pou whenua or 'land pole' on top of Mount Victoria, similar to what Americans or Canadians would call a totem pole. This, too, is part of the Te Ara o ngā Tūpuna heritage trail.

On the top of 'Mount Vic' there's also also a huge cannon and a triangular monument to the Antarctic explorer William Byrd.

Some scenes from the *Lord of the Rings* films, notably the one in which Frodo and his companions are hiding from the ringwraiths, were filmed in the Wellington Town Belt: in the wilds of downtown Wellington in effect.

Nearby Oriental Bay is a famous city beach, New Zealand's answer to Bondi Beach in Australia, though with less surf!

The city is very arty and has a lot of festivals including the World of WearableArt festival (**worldofwearableart.com**).

You can do tours of Parliament, and perhaps even see New Zealand's Prime Minister Jacinda Ardern in action. For inquiries that can't be solved in any other way, the national headquarters of the Department of Conservation is also located in downtown Wellington. It's important to call ahead, of course, using the contacts in Chapter One.

Also located downtown is the National War Memorial, described here: **mch.govt.nz/pukeahu/park/national-war-memorial**. This is not the same as the Wellington Cenotaph, a statue of a man on horseback opposite the railway station, but much grander still.

As in Auckland, there are lots of ferry services to isolated suburbs and to the South Island, and also to Matiu / Somes Island, the local equivalent of Alcatraz, once used to isolate prisoners of war and people needing quarantine.

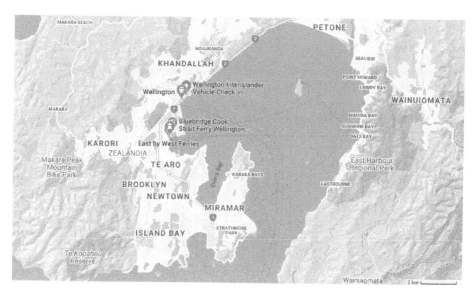

***Wellington Harbour and South Island Ferries**. Matiu / Somes Island is in the northern part of the harbour. Map data ©2020 Google.*

Wellington's Extraordinary Ecosanctuary

What's perhaps most amazing in Wellington is the Zealandia Ecosanctuary, also known as Te Māra o Tāne, the garden of the forest god Tāne. If you look very closely in the map above, you can see the word 'Zealandia' between the suburbs of Karori and Te Aro. This is a 're-wilded' nature reserve which begins only one kilometre from downtown Wellington. It's fenced off with a pest-proof fence and is full of exotic creatures like the flightless blue takahē and the tuatara.

And also the kākā, which are fairly common around the ecosanctuary now, almost to the point of being a bit of a nuisance to some homeowners who they wake up in the morning by squawking and playing on the roof.

The ecosanctuary was established on site of an old town reservoir, so there's a couple of lakes there, one of them with the old 1870s reservoir control building still.

The site of an old gold mine, now defunct, is also inside the modern ecosanctuary.

Male Auckland Tree Wētā (H. thoracica) on a leaf. Photo by James O'Hanlon, 5 November 2016, CC-BY-4.0 *via Wikimedia Commons.*

You can go for a walk through the tunnels of the mine, which for some people would take courage as they are infested with another exotic local creature called the wētā.

Like really monstrous wasps, complete with what looks like long stingers on the rear of many of them, the wētā exist in heaving masses in dark corners. It's the sort of insect that inspired the monster in *Alien*.

Well of course the old-time miners braved worse perils. For the secret is that in spite of its appearance the wētā is just about completely harmless (though it can give you a bit of a nip). As for the long 'stingers', these are what the females lay eggs through. But only in rotten logs and things like that, don't worry!

And yes, they are mostly pretty gigantic. So, it's a good thing they are harmless.

Film-maker Peter Jackson's Weta Workshop, of *Lord of the Rings* fame, is named after the wētā.

The Wild Coasts

On the south coast of Wellington, you can also see seals and penguins that have swum all the way up from Antarctica, more or less. There are signs on the winding coastal roads that tell people to beware of penguins crossing!

The west coast of New Zealand is the wild one, pummelled by westerly winds and waves, with the mountains above extra-steep and plunging directly into the sea. This made it very difficult to build roads. The road along the coast out of Wellington is called the Centennial Highway because it was only completed as late as 1940, the centenary of the signing of the Treaty of Waitangi.

But they did a good job. It's surely one of the great seaside drives of the world. Driving the Centennial Highway, it's hard not to think of the old Quincy Jones track from the original *Italian Job*, 'On Days like These'.

There's a really good walking track through these hills, too, from Paekakariki to the more distant commuter town of Paraparaumu. Both of these are railway stops and so you can catch the train from downtown Wellington to one end of the track, and then back to town from the other.

The Centennial Highway with Kāpiti Island in the background, published in the 'New Zealand Free Lance', 13 July 1949. Official credit: Raine, William Hall, 1892–1955. Centennial Highway, Wellington region – Photograph taken by William Hall Raine. Ref: PAColl-8983–67. Alexander Turnbull Library, Wellington, New Zealand. /records/22898322

It's called the Escarpment Track, escarpment being a polite word for 'cliff'. Signs at the start warn you it might be a bit scary.

The track is ten kilometres long and reminiscent of Himalayan tramping trails in places, especially the rickety-swing bridge-over-yawning chasm bits. A lot of people don't do swing bridges over chasms, of course.

Things get a bit easier toward the ends, where there are also signs pointing to revegetation projects and traditional Māori gardens.

There are also signs and picnic areas at the top, from which the sea looks like blue concrete.

When it comes to walking, there are also plenty of tracks within the city itself.

Between the inner city and the outer suburbs, you can also visit Ōtari / Wilton's Bush, a '6-star garden of international significance'. Prize specimens including an 800-year-old giant Rimu tree.

Here's a guide to Wellington Regional Trails, which describes the Escarpment Track, among others: **wellingtonregionaltrails.com.**

Kāpiti island is a really important nature reserve, as is the smaller, flatter Mana Island a little further south. You can travel to Kāpiti Island from Paraparaumu and stay overnight as a part of a guided eco-tour by Kāpiti Island Nature Tours, an organisation jointly controlled by local Māori iwi and DOC.

Further north along the coast, Ōtaki is an important centre of Māori culture. Founded in 1886, the Ōtaki-Māori Racing Club is the only Māori-owned horse-racing club in New Zealand, and one of the few indigenous horse-racing clubs in the world. Te Wānanga o Raukawa is a Māori university based at Ōtaki.

The town is also the site of Rangiātea Church, the oldest Māori Anglican church in New Zealand, built between 1849 and 1851. The church was completely rebuilt after being burned down by an arsonist in 1995.

A town you never get tired of

And so, to sum up, I never get tired of visiting Wellington and its environs, and you should go there too, when you can. But you might well experience an earth tremor or two, and you should check the weather forecast before doing anything adventurous, such as the Escarpment Track!

In the next few chapters, I carry on up the west coast north of Wellington toward the plains of the Manawatū, to Whanganui, and ultimately to Taranaki.

Blog post with more images:

a-maverick.com/blog/wild-weird-windy-wellington-new-zealands-capital-city-at-the-head-of-mauis-fish

TOUR 7: The Manawatū, Whanganui City and Taranaki

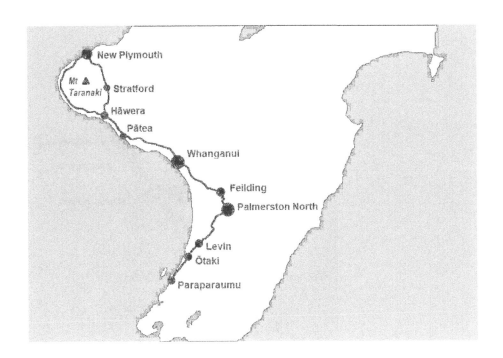

The south-western part of the North Island of New Zealand, north of Wellington. *Abbreviations are PN for the city of Palmerston North, and T for Mount Tongariro, N for Mount Ngāuruhoe and R for Mount Ruapehu. Green shows forested areas.*

CHAPTER TWENTY-NINE

From Chasms to Coast: A landscape less often travelled

THE LANDSCAPE north of Wellington, on the west side, is often overlooked by tourists and travellers. But it shouldn't be.

Check out this scene, for instance.

Rangiwahia Track Bridge in the Iron Gates area. *Image reproduced from the media gallery of CEDA, the Central Districts Economic Development Agency, ManawatuNZ.co.nz.*

It's part of a jumble of chasms called the Iron Gates, near the tiny town of Mangaweka, north-east of Palmerston North. From the Iron Gates you can look out over all the plains, with stunning views.

And there are other mighty gorges, such as the Manawatū Gorge that I will have more to say about below.

The region north of Ōtaki is wrapped around a huge bay called the South Taranaki Bight, which also means that there are plenty of beaches, mostly of a wild and lonesome sort.

'The Beauty of the South'

Heading north through Ōtaki, Levin's the first big town you get to. The town is beside two lakes named Horowhenua – the wider region around Levin is also called the Horowhenua – and Papaitonga.

Horowhenua means 'quaking ground' and refers to the rather swampy character of this part of New Zealand, which had an important flax industry at one time.

Papaitonga is the smaller of the two lakes but perhaps the most unusual. It's been preserved with all the native bush around it intact in the form of the Papaitonga Scenic Reserve.

Sometime around the end of the 1800s the politician, poet and conservationist William Pember Reeves wrote a poem about the lake's preservation, containing the line "Yet in this sacred wood no axe shall ring," and, fortunately, it's still that way.

The lake is also known as Waiwiri or 'trembling waters'.

The Town of Forest Glades

There are also several other reserves of conserved lowland rain forest around Levin. The other surviving remnants of lowland native rainforest, or 'bush', around Levin include Prouse Bush Reserve, Waiopehu Scenic Reserve (probably the most famous), Gladstone Reserve, and Kimberley Reserve.

Levin itself is in a locality originally named Taitoko, meaning sunbeam or ray of light. Perhaps the word referred to dappled glades in which the taitoko streamed through all those ancient, misty forests. These days, there's growing agitation to restore the name of Taitoko, at least as an alternative official name in the government gazette.

Levin, or Taitoko / Levin as it may soon be officially known, is also close to the northern foothills of the Tararua Ranges: a name that refers either to a spear tip ('tara') broken in two ('rua'), or to the two wives of an ancestor named Whātonga.

According to Te Ara, the online encyclopaedia of New Zealand, the Ngāti Toa iwi, who migrated to the region from the Waikato about two hundred years ago under the leadership of a warlord named Te Rauparaha during a disturbed period of history known as the Musket Wars, and who came into conflict with Horowhenua and Whanganui Māori as a result, also had their own name for the range, born of an eventual peace treaty with the Ngāti Kahungunu who lived to the east:

"... the Ngāti Toa people named the Tararua Range as Te Tuarātapu-o-Te Rangihaeata – the sacred back of Te Rangihaeata (a Ngāti Toa leader). The naming followed a peace pact between Ngāti Toa on one side of the range and Ngāti Kahungunu on the other."

But Tararua is the name that has stuck. A number of well-known tramping routes in the Tararua start out from Levin, some via the town's own bush reserves. So, you can just put down your coffees in town, strap on packs, and start tramping.

Levin's quite friendly, and I know some people who live there. But in terms of planning it leaves a bit to be desired, as it simply straggles along the main road, State Highway One. The city of Palmerston North and the town of Feilding, which I am coming to shortly, were laid out in much grander terms.

In the meantime, here are some useful resources.

Horowhenua District Council: Parks, Reserves and Recreation. Perhaps the best one-stop introduction to places to visit in the Horowhenua.

manawatuNZ.co.nz. One of the best and certainly most media-friendly tourism websites I've seen, with all sorts of travel tips and a link to a huge gallery of free, professionally shot photographs and videos to illustrate any talk or article about the Manawatū and Whanganui areas.

irongates.co.nz. A very detailed website about the little-known but remarkable Iron Gates area.

The land of heart-stopping floods

North from the Horowhenua, you enter a larger region called the Manawatū. This word means 'heart stood still'. According to Māori tradition, the name was given by an early Polynesian explorer of the new land named Haunui, or Hau.

Manawatū was bestowed by Hau after he arrived at the mouth of this river, which filled him with trepidation at the prospect of having to cross it. A river and a district known ever after for that sentiment.

Perhaps it was in flood at the time. The Manawatū is known for heart-stopping floods that spill all over the plains west of the Gorge. These are likely to get worse with global warming.

The biggest city in the area is Palmerston North: a planned city built around a vast square two hundred metres on a side, with four avenues radiating away from the Square at right angles. Prudently, it's a bit above the river.

The latest is He Ara Kotahi, a green commuter pathway with a lovely pedestrian bridge across the Manawatū river and an amazing elevated walkway through native bush as well, at Keebles Bush Crossing.

He Ara Kotahi, meaning a path of union, opened in 2019.

A couple of sections of the pathway are lit by glowing spheres in the ground, which create an impression like glow-worms.

A short distance northward on State Highway 3, Feilding's a prosperous country town that's long been important for its saleyards, a slice of New Zealand as it used to be in the days when the country was said to live 'on the sheep's back'. Feilding still does.

Feilding has a lot of surviving colonial-era gingerbread architecture. The Feildingites are very much into keeping it up, and the town's won New Zealand's annual most beautiful town award sixteen times.

It isn't too gentrified though. I went into Murphy's Bar where you can get steak for NZ $10, and then visited a friend of mine who has a grassrootsy little shop there, selling crystals.

The Chasms of the Rangītikei

Past Feilding, you pass through a transitional sort of a region known as the Rangitīkei, after its great river.

Trains unexpectedly fly off the edges of the chalk cliffs on narrow viaducts in ways that make your heart jump the first time.

It's in this area that you find the Iron Gates, with which the present chapter began.

Rātana

In the 1920s, a Māori religious and social movement took root and soon became hugely influential. This was Rātana, named after its founder Tahupōtiki Wiremu Rātana. Rātana actually became a force to be reckoned with in mainstream twentieth century Parliamentary politics. An electoral alliance between Rātana and the New Zealand Labour Party was sealed in 1935.

The deal helped to keep Labour in power for fourteen years, until 1949.

Today, the base of the Rātana movement is the Rātana Pā, some twenty kilometres south-east of Whanganui. You can visit it on the way north to Whanganui.

Blog post with more images:

a-maverick.com/blog/from-chasms-to-coast-a-landscape-less-often-travelled

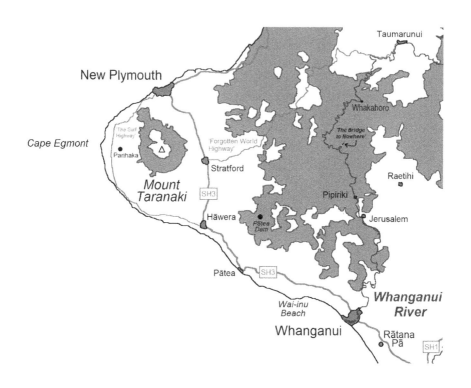

CHAPTER THIRTY

The Fascinating City of Whanganui

A S FOR the city of Whanganui, what is it famous for? Well, let's think of the thing you might least expect perhaps in such an out-of-the-way, somewhat wild locality: the <u>Serjeant Gallery</u>. First opened in 1919, it's the most significant art gallery in provincial New Zealand.

Whanganui seemed like a really depressed city to me when I visited it some years ago, but it's since revived tremendously in ways that the spruce-up of the Serjeant Gallery are a sign of.

The i-Site is really amazing, with a café, and art exhibits upstairs, and is the perfect place to find out about everything to do in the region, including nearby lakes and beaches.

Across the river from downtown Whanganui, there's the clifftop suburb of Durie Hill, from which you can have good views of the rest of the city. You can go even higher by ascending the Durie Hill War Memorial Tower, which commemorates the First World War in a most striking fashion (there's also a more conventional cenotaph downtown).

The official tourism website for Whanganui is Visit Whanganui: **visitwhanganui.nz**. Visit Whanganui has videos describing Durie Hill and other sights, among a wealth of other information.

The other impressive thing about Durie Hill is that the easiest way to get there is on foot, via a public elevator, which involves walking into the cliff through a tunnel and then riding the elevator to the top.

Nearby is Pūtiki Marae, the main marae or meeting-place of Whanganui-area lowland Māori on the site of their ancestral village or pā which was also called Pūtiki, and another suburban hill called Korokota, Māori for Golgotha, because when the Reverend Richard Taylor arrived to perform missionary work in 1843 there were still bones lying around the base of the hill from the hundreds who had lost their lives when the settlement was attacked in 1829 by forces of the warlord Te Rauparaha, who was mentioned in the last chapter.

The Reverend Taylor arranged for the bones to be buried. Before acquiring its new missionary name, the hill had been known as Taumata Karoro.

A restored paddle steamer called the *Waimarie,* or peaceful waters, still plies the lower reaches of the Whanganui River for the tourists.

You can also go for a ride on a restored upriver tunnel boat, a sort of early jetboat called the *Wairua* ('spirit'). It's smaller than the *Waimarie,* but faster, as you'd expect.

Travelling on the *Wairua* must be an almost unique technological experience in the 21st century, if not actually unique.

The fact that it's powered by a Diesel these days doesn't make the Wairua inauthentic. The original steam engine was abandoned early on as something that was too heavy for the rapids, along with the vast amounts of coal it consumed. For most of its career the Wairua ran on a more modern sort of an engine intended to lighten it up and make it more sprightly, as befitted its name, 'spirit'. Truly, indeed, one of the first jetboats, developed by trial and error, if not the first.

Whanganui has vintage weekends in which the *Waimarie* and *Wairua* sail up and down the river while a steam train crosses the river's railway bridge and biplanes flit about. They do the steampunk thing in Oamaru, but this is for real. Bring your goggles!

Coda: Wai-inu Beach

As you travel north out of Whanganui and cross the invisible frontier into the Taranaki region, the very first place you come to is the town of Waitotara and, to the left, Wai-inu Beach. This is worth remembering because not only is it an attractive beach but also, it's an approved freedom camping area that you can make into your base for exploring the city of Whanganui, if you plan to be there for a night or more and are keen to save as much money as possible.

Blog post with more images:

a-maverick.com/blog/union-jacks-and-grumpy-cats-conflict-over-monuments-in-aotearoa-new-zealand

CHAPTER THIRTY-ONE

Lands of the Shining Peak: 'When death itself is dead, I shall be alive'

ANOTHER important region of the North Island is Taranaki, also known as the Taranaki or, very colloquially, the Naki.

Everyone in the region lives under the beautiful 2,518 metre (8,261 feet) volcano that gives the region its name, Mount Taranaki: a name that's thought to mean 'shining peak', a reference to the way the mountain looks during the cooler months of the year.

The area around Mount Taranaki is mostly green farmland, apart from a national park which takes in the volcano in an almost circular fashion, plus a couple of eroded volcanic peaks to its northwest, Pouakai and Kaitake.

Officially, the Taranaki Region of New Zealand extends from Waitotara in the south to Mokau in the north. About two thirds of the region's population of just over 122,000 lives in the city of New Plymouth and its surrounding district, which have, altogether, a population of 84,400.

The western part of the Taranaki Region consists almost entirely of the slopes and lower slopes of Mount Taranaki and the adjacent peaks.

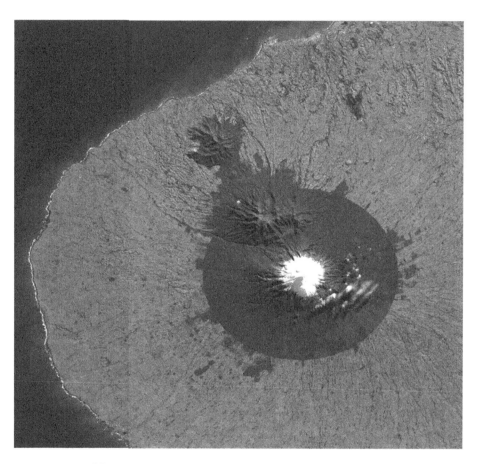

Mt Taranaki and Environs, including the port city of New Plymouth due north of the peak. *ASTER image 27 May 2001. NASA public domain image record 3000/3881/egmont_ast_2001086 via the NASA Earth Observatory.*

Mount Taranaki. *Whites Aviation Ltd., 1969: Photographs. Ref: WA-68672-F. Alexander Turnbull Library, Wellington, New Zealand. /records/22305211*

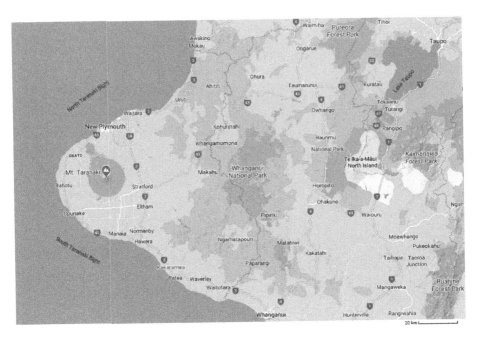

The Taranaki Region in relation to the central North Island. Map data ©2020 Google.

Tourism resources for Taranaki include the official tourism website Taranaki Like No Other, **visit.taranaki.info** and the independent things-to-do guide Hello Taranaki (website and app), **hellotaranaki.co.nz**.

The present cone of Mount Taranaki is only a bit over three thousand years old, and last erupted about 250 years ago.

It's the latest in a long string of pretty-looking volcanoes that have grown up on more or less the same spot and then blown their top like Mount St Helens.

Scientists predict that today's Mount Taranaki will vanish in a puff of smoke itself one day.

In the meantime, we can enjoy scenic postcard views of the beautiful mountain from almost every angle, while it's still there!

The spot on which the city of New Plymouth is established is called Ngāmotu, meaning 'the islands' in Māori. That's because there are several offshore islands, the eroded remains of an extinct volcano themselves.

These are called Ngā Motu or the Sugar Loaf Islands, and the city's most central beach is called Ngāmotu Beach.

Ngāmotu is often used as an alternative name for New Plymouth city, for instance on the council website, though at present it's not official.

There are lots of other famous vantage-points, such as Lake Mangamahoe, where you can get a view of the mountain reflected in the water.

I travelled north along the coast from Whanganui to get to the Taranaki: ironically following the route of Whanganui settlers and their local Māori allies who invaded in the late 1860s in the form of the Pātea Field Force, named after the village of Pātea which they occupied and took over.

There were at least three wars in the Taranaki between 1860 and 1870 and some relics of the wars remain.

The battleground that's become a campground

One of the most famous or notorious battles of the South Taranaki wars was fought at a place called Te Ngutu o te Manu, meaning 'the beak of the bird'. There, Gustavus von Tempsky, the Prussian-born commander of a unit called the Forest Rangers, met his end along with about eighteen other settler militiamen under his command and an unknown number of Māori allies (kūpapa), when they were ambushed in a clearing by anti-government Māori.

The ambushers were led by a skilled strategist named Riwha Tītokowaru, who had prepared a trap and lured von Tempsky's column into it.

Though it wasn't the biggest battle ever fought on New Zealand soil, Te Ngutu o te Manu was very demoralising for the settlers.

For von Tempsky was perhaps New Zealand's first celebrity, a man who struck dashing poses before the camera. Small copies of these photographs, known as cartes-de-visite, were handed out like modern business cards.

The site of the battle is now a historical reserve about two kilometres from the town of Kapuni by road, past the water treatment plant on Skeet Road and about half a kilometre down Ahipaipa Road. While the rest of the country nearby has been cleared for farming, the clearing where the ambush occurred continues to be surrounded by forest. So, you can't miss it.

You can even camp in the clearing. That's if the whole idea doesn't strike you as a bit freaky. Then again, there's always a ghost-free motel up the road.

Remember Parihaka!

Taranaki Māori lost a lot of land to the eventually victorious New Zealand Government, which settled large numbers of European farmers in the Taranaki region. Taranaki Māori were more seriously affected by land confiscation than any other group.

Past Hāwera, there are two ways to get to New Plymouth. I decided to take State Highway 45, known as the Surf Highway because there are lots of good surfing beaches on Taranaki's wild western extremity.

But the real reason I took the highway was because I wanted to visit <u>Parihaka</u>, the site of a famous act of nonviolent resistance in 1881 which is honoured on the website of the Gandhi Foundation, and may actually have helped to inspire the great Indian peaceful resister personally.

Parihaka is close to the westernmost extremity of Taranaki, an extremity known as Cape Egmont.

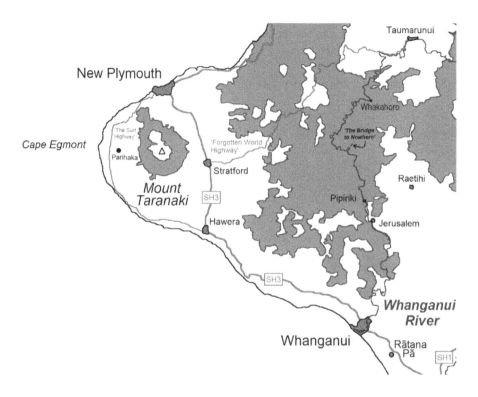

Until quite recently the mountain itself was also known as Mount Egmont. The mountain has now reverted to its older Māori name officially, though Egmont is still used in technical circles so as not to confuse foreign scientists who know the mountain by that name.

West of SH 45, a local road called Cape Road runs down to Cape Egmont, which has a lighthouse you can photograph in the same frame as Mount Taranaki.

About 200 metres before Cape Road, on the right, is Mid-Parihaka Road. This leads to Parihaka Pā, where in 1881 a group of Māori led by Te Whiti-o-Rongomai III, and Tohu Kākahi,

312

ploughed the land to demonstrate that they did not recognise its earlier confiscation by the New Zealand Government.

A BLOODLESS CONTEST.

A WRETCHED FIASCO.

ARREST OF TE WHITI AND TOHU.

THE NATIVES PEACEFUL.

HOW OUR CORRESPONDENTS FOILED MR BRYCE.

THE WHOLE SCENE WATCHED BY HIDDEN WITNESSES.

NOBLE ATTITUDE OF TE WHITI.

[BY TELEGRAPH.]

[FROM OUR OWN CORRES-PONDENT.]

PUNGAREHU, Nov. 5.

The Lyttelton Star*'s take on the story,* from From Vincent O'Malley, 'The Invasion of Parihaka, 5 November 1881: An Eyewitness Account', 5 November 2012, on The Meeting Place – A New Zealand History Blog. The Star's correspondent styled Bryce as "the generalissimo."

Te Whiti and Tohu were joined by Riwha Tītokowaru, the same commander who had defeated von Tempsky at Te Ngutu o te Manu.

Te Whiti, Tohu and Tītokowaru were imprisoned, released, and legally harrassed for the next few years. On the previous page, there's a photo of a sketch I saw in New Plymouth's amazing Puke Ariki ('hill of the high chief') museum showing Tītokowaru and Te Whiti in the dock at one of their trials.

Tītokowaru and Te Whiti in the dock

Te Whiti and Tītokowaru were quite humble people and did not like to have their pictures made.

The idea of peaceful resistance may have been inspired by the pacifist customs of the Moriori, a related ethnic group who live on the Chatham Islands east of New Zealand. The Moriori were violently conquered and enslaved by earlier Taranaki Māori in the 1830s but continued to resist peacefully. I talk about this in another blog post, which I will link to at the end of this chapter.

Both Tohu and Tītokowaru were buried, when their time came, at secret locations. The saying that 'over a seaman's grave there bloom no roses' also applies to Tohu and Tītokowaru as far as memorials go.

The fifth of November would be celebrated by the colonists as Guy Fawkes Day, as it is in England. But not as Parihaka Day, as the settlers soon forgot about the whole thing once they felt safe.

For a time, it seemed as though Tītokowaru's promise to his followers would be rendered hollow:

"I shall not die

"I shall not die

"When death itself is dead, I shall be alive."

Amnesia lasted until the first publication of the Palmerston North-born historian Dick Scott's book *Ask that Mountain* in 1975.

Blog posts (with more images)

a-maverick.com/blog/lands-of-the-shining-peak-when-death-itself-is-dead-i-shall-be-alive

a-maverick.com/blog/east-to-the-chathams

CHAPTER THIRTY-TWO

Climbing the Cone of Catastrophes

I'VE CLIMBED Mount Taranaki twice, via the Northern Summit Route which starts near New Plymouth and via the Southern Summit Route which starts at Dawson Falls.

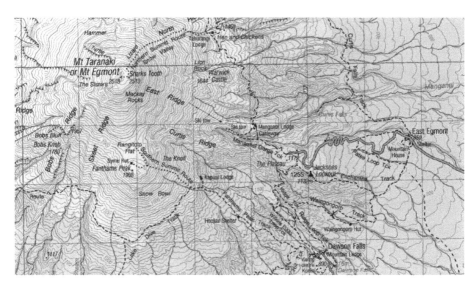

Mount Taranaki summit and Fanthams Peak plus Dawson Falls and East Egmont. Map data by LINZ via NZ Topo Map, 2020.

You get to Dawson Falls from the town of Stratford. And from there also to East Egmont and the East Ridge, where there's a club skifield called the Manganui Ski Area. It's beside the Manganui Gorge, which is sometimes filled in with snow from avalanches: a sobering sight.

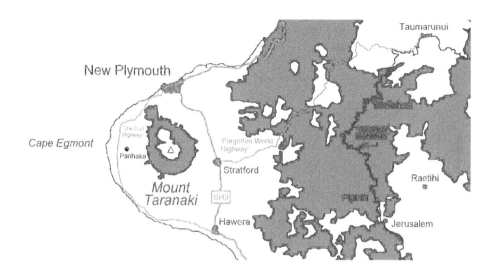

The Cone of Catastrophes

There are three other things to realise about climbing the mountain now once more called Taranaki, all of which can be summed up by the word 'exposure'.

The first is weather. In spite of all those scenic views of the mountain against blue sky, *on* at least two days out of three, Mount Taranaki is wrapped in cloud.

The second is that Mount Taranaki is quite steep almost everywhere, with lots of bluffs. There's a good risk of a bad fall if you slip or get lost in the clouds.

The third is that there isn't really anywhere to hide from bad weather in most places. The steepness of the mountain means that the snow doesn't build up to any great thickness before avalanching off, and so it can be hard to dig a snow cave or to improvise any kind of igloo-type shelter from bad weather. And there's not too many places to hide from avalanches either.

More than eighty climbers have died on the slopes of Mount Taranaki since the first recorded instance of such a fatality in the 1890s. To which must be added the victims of the several aircraft that have crashed into the prominent peak in bad weather and darkness as well.

For all these reasons, Mount Taranaki's been dubbed 'the cone of catastrophes'.

Having said all that, between six and eight thousand people were climbing Mount Taranaki each year a decade ago. And perhaps as many as fifteen thousand each year now.

To be on the safe side, climbing the mountain's generally only regarded as advisable from January through to April, when there is isn't much snow or ice to slip on, and when there's also less chance of bad weather on a day that starts out fine.

Even on the hottest days there is still a bit of snow and ice right at the top. So, you do get to see some, at least.

The Northern Summit Route: How I first got to the top

The first time I tried climbing Mount Taranaki was via the Northern Summit Route. We passed the Taranaki Alpine Club's Tahurangi Lodge, about one and half hours in from the road end, and got onto the steep scree (loose gravel) slopes.

Climbing in scree above the low New Zealand treeline is really quite difficult, because for every step up, you slide back at least half of it in the loose ground, so it's just a constant up-and-down battle to make even a few metres.

We finally made it up onto the Lizard, a more stable rocky ridge, and then from there it was only another few hundred metres of climbing to the summit. We stopped for a short break after the exhausting scree slopes, then carried on to the summit. I enjoyed the tramp, and the view from the top of Mt Taranaki was beautiful – over the clouds we could even see the distant Mt Ruapehu.

Here's a DOC webpage on places to go in Taranaki, which includes a link to the Northern Summit Route, which it calls Mount Taranaki Summit Track: **doc.govt.nz/parks-and-recreation/places-to-go/taranaki**. The page also includes information about other hikes and walks and is well worth looking up in its entirety.

The almost perfect cone of Mount Taranaki

A view of the Tongariro National Park volcanoes in the distance from Mount Taranaki

Mount Taranaki from the air, Fanthams Peak in the foreground

The Orphan all alone

Stratford's also a good place from which to view the largest of Mount Taranaki's side-peaks, Fanthams Peak or Panitahi, which is 1,966 metres high. It's on the southern side of Mount Taranaki and much closer to the summit than either Pouakai or Kaitake, which are actually the remains of older volcanoes.

The name Panitahi means an orphan all alone. The name Fanthams Peak honours Fanny Fantham who in 1887, at the age of nineteen, became the first woman known for certain to have climbed Panitahi. She climbed it as part of a mixed party of about fourteen men and women hoping to get to the summit by way of Dawson Falls.

Most soon fell behind, including all the women apart from Fanny Fantham. Eventually, Fanny and four men made it to the top of Panitahi. After some cheering the men decided to rename it Fantham's Peak in her honour.

In Fanny Fantham's Footsteps

The second time I went up, the objective was to climb Taranaki via Fanthams Peak.

I looked in the New Zealand Alpine Club journals for information about the east side of Mount Taranaki and found that there was a lodge, the Kapuni Lodge, owned by the Mount Egmont Alpine Club only an hour further up the mountain from the Dawson Falls carpark and visitor centre where these more southern routes generally start out from. Like the geologists the club has kept the old name so far, presumably to differentiate itself from the Mount Taranaki Alpine Club on the north side!

The visitor centre, carpark and falls are at 902 metres, which is a fair way up the mountain already, and yet only a half-hour drive from Stratford.

We rang the club and managed to book the hut. We set off, tramping, at ten o'clock and made it to the hut at eleven. We were let into the beautiful Kapuni Lodge by the chairperson of the Mount Egmont Alpine Club.

As the chairperson showed us around the hut, she told us to take care on the mountain. We fell to talking about the mountain's latest casualties, two climbers who'd been caught in bad weather.

(Four years later, in October 2017, the New Zealand news media website **stuff.co.nz** published an in-depth online story about the tragedy, called 'Too high, too late, two dead' was published. It's freely available to all.)

We stayed the night in Kapuni Lodge and left at eight o'clock the next morning to climb to the summit.

After a while he decided to go back to the lodge. I followed the trail a few hours on up to Syme Hut on Fanthams Peak, named after the founder of the Mount Egmont Alpine Club. Syme Hut was first built in 1930 by the club, before being replaced in 1980 by the current DOC hut.

The grassy slopes heading up towards the summit

Fanthams Peak with Syme Hut visible on the near-side crater rim

The Mount Egmont Alpine Club website includes a link to a silent 1930 film about the opening of the original Syme Hut, which the film calls "new."

Check out the scene at about 3 minutes in, called 'A precarious vantage point atop Fantham's Peak' – I wonder if it's still there?

From Fanthams Peak you cross the Rangitoto Flat and then proceed on up to the summit of Mount Taranaki. I had to use my ice axe on the rocks; a technique known as dry-tooling.

The view was beautiful, especially looking up toward the Taranaki summit.

One of the really conspicuous features that you can see from the mountain is the circular edge of the national park, known as Egmont National Park till recently but now called Te Papakura o Taranaki.

I lost my breath getting up but made it to the top. I looked down and saw that the clouds were coming in fast towards the mountain.

But I didn't want to linger, for fear of the tendrils of mist that seemed to be feeling their way toward me as if they were alive. All those stories about bad weather had me pretty freaked!

Blog post with more images:

a-maverick.com/blog/climbing-the-cone-of-catastrophes

CHAPTER THIRTY-THREE

The Talents of Taranaki

IN THE last two chapters I've dwelt on the history of Taranaki, and the region's famous mountain. But what of its other attractions?

Pātea

This small town is famous for the Pātea Māori Club's catchy song called *Poi E*, released on vinyl in 1984 and the first Māori-language song to get to the top of the hit parade in New Zealand.

The story's all the more remarkable because the song was considered too offbeat and ethnic to get any airplay on the radio, at first.

Well, the fact that the song was a huge hit *anyway* quite literally ended that era overnight and put modern Māori music on the map. The song even wound up on a British variety show.

Which was, apparently, the sort of thing the Queen liked to watch. And so, next minute, the Pātea Māori Club were invited to give what the British call a Royal Command Performance. But the New Zealand Government refused to help pay their passage. The musicians scraped up the money themselves rather than disappoint the Queen, and went.

A good documentary about the making of *Poi E* and its times came out in 2016. It would make a terrific feature film but so far that hasn't happened. I rather suspect it would make New Zealand's politicians squirm, even today.

Eight kilometres northbound out of Pātea on State Highway 3, Ball Road takes you inland to the Pātea Dam. As you cross the Patea River for the first time some 18 km up the road, the road changes its name to Maben Road and then continues another 10 km to the dam.

The Pātea Dam is 82 metres high and located in the same general wilderness as the upper Whanganui River, except that it's on the Pātea River. The lake behind the dam, Lake Rotorangi, is 46 km long, the longest artificial lake in New Zealand. There's a freedom camping spot at the dam and a pleasant bushwalk that involves going across the dam.

Hāwera

There's an amazing amount of talent that comes out of even some of the smaller towns in New Zealand: not always appreciated locally. For instance, a bit further up the State Highway 3, at Hāwera, there once lived an author named Ronald Hugh Morrieson.

Morrieson's novels were about an imaginary small town populated by all sorts of more or less absurd characters.

Morrieson was still fairly obscure when he died in 1972 after having complained to another writer that he hoped he wasn't one of those blighters [i.e., people; he actually used a cruder expression] who only got to be famous after they were dead. From which springs the title of a surreal docu-drama made about him ten years after he died, called *One of those Blighters.*

That was around the time that his books were starting to be made into feature films, of which the funniest is probably *Came a Hot Friday* (1984).

In 1992, with Morrieson about as posthumously famous as he'd feared, the local council decided it was time to have his house knocked down and replaced with a Kentucky Fried Chicken restaurant.

Protests from the world of literature and film were to no avail. For apparently, there were still people in Hāwera who thought Morrieson's novels were about them!

Lucys Gully and the Kaitake and Pouakai Ranges

As you come around the corner from Cape Egmont, there's a spot near the seaside town of Ōakura where the Surf Highway brushes against the former Egmont National Park, now Te Papakura o Taranaki. There are a whole lot of really good daywalks in the bush at this spot.

Lucys Gully is a picnic spot closest to the road, where American redwoods sprout from an understory of giant New Zealand tree ferns, just as they do at Whakarewarewa.

From Lucys Gully and some other roads nearby, you can do easy walks in the Kaitake Range, which is lush and coastal.

You can also do more alpine hikes in the Pouakai Range, which take two to three days and involve staying in one of the huts on the range. These tracks are more advanced.

The best-known hut on the Pouakai Range is Pouakai Hut. It's actually the most popular hut in the national park even though it isn't on Mount Taranaki. And that's because it's so close to the coast, with epic views of the coastal plains, New Plymouth and the Tasman Sea, far below.

Pouakai Hut. Photo by Tamsen Walker from DOC Pouakai Hut brochure, CC-BY-4.0.

Down on the coast, it's worth visiting Ōakura Beach, from which you can get a good view of the dramatic natural skyline produced by the 156-metre Paritutu Rock and Ngā Motu ('the islands'), also known as the Sugar Loaf Islands. These are essentially the same as the steep mountains that dominate the skyline of Rio de Janeiro, although the ones in Rio are bigger.

At Ōakura, these amazing natural features are on your right when you face out to sea. In New Plymouth, they are on your left.

Ōakura Beach, photo by 'RealCaptainUltra', 25 October 2019, CC-BY-SA 4.0 via Wikimedia Commons

The sand is black. That's common along of the west coast of New Zealand on both main islands, though the exact substance that makes the sand black changes from place to place. In Taranaki it's a volcanic mineral, as you'd expect.

You can climb Paritutu Rock for some amazing views, though it's apparently a bit intrepid and I've not yet done it.

New Plymouth

Also known in Māori as Ngāmotu after the islands, New Plymouth is a beautiful, modern city which is all the more beautiful for being under Mount Taranaki as well as beside the sea.

New Plymouth looking towards Ōakura. *From the Photo Gallery of <u>VisitNewPlymouth</u>.*

New Plymouth has always been a thrilling sort of place, into which the locals have for a long time put in a lot of effort in terms of civic beautification.

Pukekura Park is one of the best parks anywhere: a really magical place organised around a sort of ravine or grotto in the middle of the city with a lake in the middle, spanned by the Poet's Bridge. You can hire little rowboats for about NZ $10 for half an hour. In addition to being very restful, rowing up and down the lake is also the only way to get this classic shot.

The Poet's Bridge in Pukekura Park with Mount Taranaki peeping over the top. Photo by Te Kaunihera-ā-Rohe o Ngāmotu/New Plymouth District Council.

But be warned that there won't be any snow to speak of in high summer. These are more spring/autumn/fine day in winter shots.

You might ask why the snow-capped peak of Mount Taranaki seems to rise out of a tropical jungle.

The answer is that, in the Southern Hemisphere, the sort of forest that people from the Northern Hemisphere would think of as tending to go with snow-capped mountains – oak trees, maples, and that sort of thing – never evolved to the same degree.

Instead, the plants that once populated the hot, steamy jungles of the dinosaur age simply adapted themselves to the Southern Hemisphere's cooler spots without changing outwardly.

Survival of jungle-type plants was made easier by the fact that because there is more water and less land in the Southern Hemisphere, winters in the temperate latitudes of the Southern Hemisphere tend to be less harsh than in similar latitudes of the Northern Hemisphere.

Most parts of the North Island seldom get below freezing in winter. Or not far below at any rate. And so, jungle-type vegetation survives the winter in these areas.

There's just something about the sight of the snow-capped peak of Mount Taranaki framed by plants of tropical appearance! To the Northern Hemisphere eye, it must be a curious thing.

For 180 years, now, it's been standard for painters and photographers to show Mount Taranaki with snow on top, behind some local vegetation for contrast.

Heaphy, Charles, 1820–1881. Heaphy, Charles, 1820–1881 :Mt Egmont from the southward. [September? 1840]. Ref: C-025–008. Alexander Turnbull Library, Wellington, New Zealand. /records/23173901

And there's plenty of opportunity to see scenes like that in Pukekura Park!

Within the park and its lush rain forest, there's also a natural amphitheatre called the Bowl of Brooklands where performances are held on a stage above the lake. that's just magic after dark, especially during the annual Festival of Lights.

From a downtown location close to the central city and Marsland Hill, Pukekura Park meanders about two kilometers inland in the direction of Mount Taranaki, which can be seen peeping over the park's trees and lake in the photo of the Poets' Bridge.

When WOMAD comes to New Zealand, it's held there too.

These days, New Plymouth has an amazing coastal walkway. In fact, the United Nations gave New Plymouth an award, a while back, as the world's most livable city in its size range.

If Whanganui has the Serjeant Gallery, New Plymouth has an equally famous one called the Govett-Brewster Art Gallery. These days, it has a shiny stainless-steel exterior which really has the wow factor.

The Govett-Brewster Art Gallery includes the Len Lye Centre, dedicated to the New Zealand-born artist Len Lye who lived most of his life in New York but received a lot of support from the Govett-Brewster Art Gallery in later life. Lye willed all his major works to the Govett-Brewster. Among a whole lot of other achievements, Len Lye could probably claim to have invented the 1980s rock video – except that he was making films like this in the 1930s. I've got one of these in the blog post that's linked at the end of this chapter.

The Govett-Brewster Art Gallery and Len Lye Centre, *looking northwest at dusk from Devon Street West. Photo by Sam Hartnett, reproduced with the permission of New Plymouth District Council.*

Just south of New Plymouth is Lake Mangamahoe, which has supplied many a calendar shot over the years.

New Plymouth used to be quite small and sleepy. But the region has boomed over the last fifty years on the basis of oil and gas, which was first discovered in 1915, as well as its traditional dairy farming sector (Eltham and Ōkato are major dairy factory towns). There are lots of small nodding-donkey wells even in downtown New Plymouth, and, offshore, you can see the huge Māui platform, which has been there for some decades.

Stratford and the Roads and Trails that lead around the mountain

From New Plymouth I headed down State Highway 3 to Stratford. Stratford's the place you set off for Dawson Falls / Te Rere o Noke from, and it's also got quite an interesting glockenspiel clock tower, a glockenspiel being a bit like a xylophone but with metal keys.

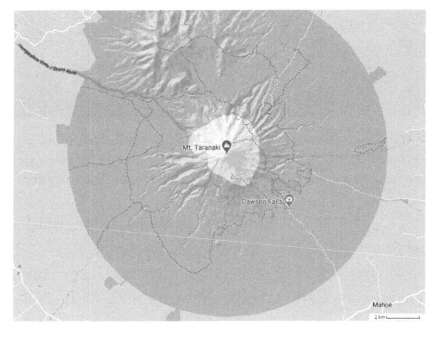

Some of the Tracks and Trails on Mount Taranaki. *Map data ©2020 Google.*

Well, anyway, if you can see that thing, you know you're in Stratford and not some other town!

Mount Taranaki is covered in tracks and trails, with the greatest concentration of them around Dawson Falls / Te Rere o Noke. Even if you've got no intention whatsoever of actually climbing the mountain, you can still enjoy yourself on these pathways.

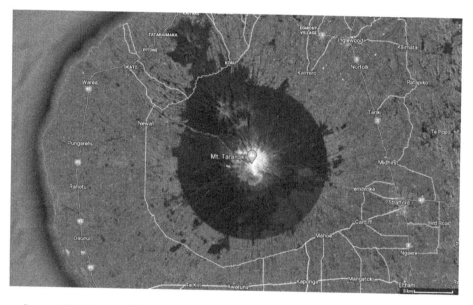

Inner Mt Taranaki Roads. *Imagery ©2020 TerraMetrics. Map Data ©2020 Google.*

Another thing you can do from Stratford is to drive around the mountain on a close-in road loop that's mostly just twelve kilometres or so from the summit. The loop road undergoes several name changes along the way. It goes right through the national park between the Kaitake and Pouakai Ranges, where it's called Carrington Road. There's a big botanical garden called <u>Pukeiti</u> on this section, at around the spot where the road bends from going northward, to going eastward.

Between Egmont Village and Inglewood, you can also take a detour toward the mountain to a place called Kaimiro, where there's a place called the VolcaNoview Tavern. Nearby, there are the Stanleigh Garden and the aptly named Berghöhen Garden, meaning 'mountain heights' in German.

People from Taranaki are very much into creating pleasant gardens, perhaps because of the example set by the remarkable Pukekura Park and also because the climate is very suitable for it. Not to mention the fact of the mountain for a backdrop, which also means that they do a roaring trade in wedding photography.

(Every spring, there is a Taranaki Garden Festival in New Plymouth as well.)

All in all, you could have a very pleasant time just puttering around the mountain, even without going up it, and discovering other attractions (these are just the ones I've noticed). And of course, it's huge when you're that close.

It's possible to go all the way around on these close-in roads and eventually back to Stratford. Which is also where State Highway 43, the Forgotten World Highway, begins, in the opposite, eastward direction to the mountain roads. I'm going to be talking about the Forgotten World Highway in the next chapter!

North via Mokau

Or, you could go north out of Taranaki the more usual way via State Highway 3. The main attractions in that direction are the Whitecliffs Walkway, Tongaporutu Beach and the wild, sweeping Mokau River.

The Whitecliffs Walkway begins at Pukearuhe at its southern end, where there is also a historic reserve dedicated to the last casualties of the war in Taranaki who were killed here in an especially regrettable incident.

The walkway ends at Tongaporutu, though the northern section of the walkway is currently closed. There is a stock tunnel, also officially closed due to safety concerns, that leads down to the beach at Te Horo, halfway along the walkway.

It's a really primordial landscape, from which you can still see Mount Taranaki, across the North Taranaki Bight. There are many scenic views along this section of coast.

Tongaporutu Beach, at the northern end of the walkway and accessible at low tide from the hamlet of Tongaporutu, has some absolutely amazing rock stacks known as the Three Sisters and Elephant Rock (which really does look like an elephant).

341

Blog post with more images:

a-maverick.com/blog/the-talents-of-taranaki

TOUR 8: The Whanganui River, Pureora and the Forgotten World

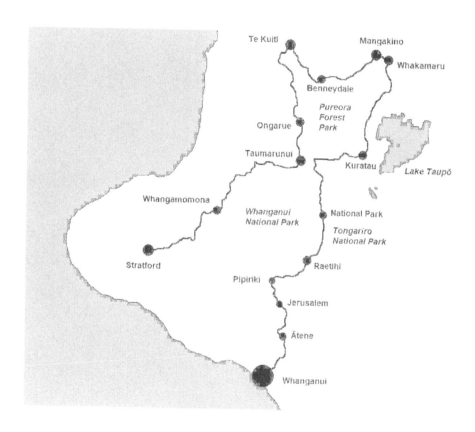

CHAPTER THIRTY-FOUR

Forgotten World: The North Island's Rugged Interior

JUST LATELY, I came across a diary of travels in old-time New Zealand called *In the Land of the Tui*. Published in London in the 1890s, the diary was kept by a woman named Eliza Wilson.

At one point, the redoubtable Mrs. Wilson mentions a curious fact that is still an aspect of New Zealand life today. After running into some Auckland polo players at Christchurch's Riccarton Racecourse, she wrote that:

"We very rarely meet any residents of Auckland so far south, and it has been pleasant to hear something of that portion of these islands which seems as remote as though it were in another sphere. It is odd that a town, so recently the seat of Government [Auckland was the capital of New Zealand from 1842 until 1865], should now have become strange to the rest of the Colony; but so it is; Wellington, Christchurch and Dunedin are always en rapport, but Auckland appears distant and separate."

There is a very good reason why this was so, and why it remains so. The reason lies in the extraordinary ruggedness of a belt of terrain that stretches all the way from Taranaki, at the westward extension of the North Island, to East Cape at its eastern-most end. This belt of rugged terrain is caused by the collision of tectonic plates, the Australian and the Pacific, and it

345

isolates Auckland from the rest of the country almost as effectively as a larger or more obvious mountain range would.

Both of the North Island's two largest rivers originate in this belt, which includes Lake Waikaremoana, Lake Taupō and the large volcanoes of the central North Island. The Waikato River flows northward from Lake Taupō to reach the sea south of Auckland. The other of these two big rivers, the Whanganui, originates near Lake Rotoaira and flows northward, then westward, and finally southward to the sea at Whanganui, a distance of 290 kilometres.

Though mainly used by cycle tourists (mountain bikes are best) the Forgotten World Highway can be driven by car; but it pays to fill up first and I wouldn't take a really flash car down that road.

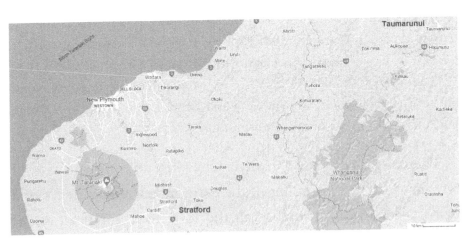

The Forgotten World Highway (SH 43) runs from Stratford to Taumarunui (names added in bold for this book). Map data ©2020 Google.

The Forgotten World Highway gets its name because it's a real back road through the hills into the central North Island. It follows the route of a railway line (used only for goods) and used to be an important pack track for moving animals in the past. Today, it's very popular with mountain bikers. Quite a lot of the highway is sealed these days as well – progress!

The Forgotten World Highway runs all the way through to Taumarunui, the same town that's the highest navigable port on the Whanganui River.

There's a lot that's truly picturesque.

The Whangamomona Hotel, Whangamomona

The Whangamomona Saddle, in the middle of the highway, is covered in tropical-looking native bush. It's close to the hamlet of Whangamomona, which styles itself as the Republic of Whangamomona because it's so remote!

The Whanganui River is popular with canoeists who paddle or float down its innumerable bends in an otherwise utterly inaccessible terrain.

As with Lake Waikaremoana, much of the North Island interior is rich in Māoritanga. And the Whanganui River is no exception.

A notoriously unsuccessful attempt to settle European farmers in this area is commemorated by the 'Bridge to Nowhere', a bridge at the end of a road that leads to – well – to what some people would consider to be nowhere.

The whole of this interior terrain, right through to the East Coast, is a site for adventures, including rafting and canoeing on wild rivers such as the Motu, which flows down to the Bay of Plenty. These rivers are shorter than the Whanganui – but they are also steeper.

Wild horses inhabit some of the more steppe-like parts of this terrain, in the vicinity of the Kaimanawa Range just east of the large volcanoes of the Tongariro National Park. From the Kaimanawa Range low mountains also run southward to form the Ruahine Range and then, south of the Manawatu Gorge where a river rises to the east of the range and flows west through a great crack in the earth, the Tararua Range and its foothills around Wellington such as the Akatarawa and the Remutaka Ranges.

For much the last 150 years, by the way, the rugged interior area west of Lake Taupō was known as the King Country, as it was an area to which the Māori King and his followers had retreated after being largely defeated in conflict with the colonists and the British, in the days of their pre-Tūrangawaewae exile. I'm not sure whether that expression is still quite as current as it used to be.

Blog post with more images:

a-maverick.com/blog/forgotten-world-the-north-islands-rugged-interior

The south-western part of the North Island of New Zealand, north of Wellington.

CHAPTER THIRTY-FIVE

Tales of the Whanganui

A HUNDRED YEARS AGO, New Zealand's rivers were highways. Back then, the Whanganui River was called the Rhine of New Zealand. Goods were shipped up and down it as far as Taumarunui, 230 kilometres (140 miles) inland from the port of Whanganui.

That was one reason the river was compared to the Rhine. The other reason was the scenery.

The "Drop Scene" Wanganui River, 1900–1910, Whanganui, by Frederick George Radcliffe, Brown & Stewart. No known copyright restrictions. Via the online collection of Te Papa, the National Museum of New Zealand, Wellington (O.031110, Purchased 2007).

Like the Manawatu and the Rangitīkei, the Whanganui cuts through gorges. Except that in the case of the Whanganui, it's pretty much gorges all the way.

The stereo image, above, shows a bend in the upper reaches of the river called Aratira or 'path of the travelling party' by Māori. Colonials called it the Drop Scene, because they thought it looked like a stage backdrop for an opera.

Group of Māori women on a road alongside the Whanganui River. Ref: 1/2–140017-F. Alexander Turnbull Library, Wellington, New Zealand. /records/22339191.

The Whanganui River also has the sites of a great many pā or Māori villages on it. Normally fortified and on a hilltop or crag, these were the equivalent of the castles of the Rhine.

A road called the Whanganui River Road runs up the east bank of the Whanganui River, as far as Pipiriki. After that, there's no more road access to the river until you get much closer to Taumarunui. The Whanganui River Road is undoubtedly the premier, scenic, riverside heritage route in New Zealand. It's a bit wider now than it used to be!

Here's a close-up detail from the last photo: I think they look pretty cool!

I went down the Whanganui River a while back, in open, Canadian-style canoes. I would paddle to the side rather than risk shooting the rapids, and even on a couple of occasions I lugged the kayak over shingle to avoid the rapids. I did it over three or four days, and it was just fantastic. There were quite a few goats on the side of the river, and it certainly was wild!

The river flows through a national park, but it is threatened by the intensification of farming all the same. It would be more at risk if the country around it wasn't so hilly. Also making things worse is the fact that water is taken from the headwaters of the Whanganui River to make hydroelectricity and not returned. I've more to say about this below.

A hundred years ago, there was a plan to settle returned soldiers from World War One in this area and to 'break in' the land, but the scheme was eventually defeated by the sheer roughness of the terrain. Not, however, before the government constructed a bridge across one of the streams that feeds into the Whanganui River in what was before, and would soon be again, the middle of nowhere.

These days, you can walk to the Bridge to Nowhere, as it's called. It carries no wheeled traffic apart from mountain bikes, perhaps, and never will.

Another famous spot on the river is Jerusalem, formerly known as Patiarero in Māori and then subsequently as Hiruhārama, which got its new name as a result of the activities of missionaries who moved up the river in the 1850s. Jerusalem later became the site of the French missionary Mother Suzanne Aubert's activities.

Mother Aubert founded the Sisters of Compassion, the only Catholic religious order founded in New Zealand, a country otherwise mostly colonised by Protestants, and is at present a candidate for canonisation.

Around the start of the 1970s a commune was also established at Jerusalem by the poet James K. Baxter, who died and was buried there in 1972.

The upper reaches of the river were at one time a stronghold of the anti-British Pai Mārire movement, which means 'good and peaceful' though in reality it soon evolved a fighting warrior sect, more commonly known in that manifestation as Hau Hau ('wind, wind') after the movement's battle cry.

Hau Hau were among the most hard-line of the various Māori groups opposed to colonists and the British in the New Zealand Wars of the 1860s. At that time Jerusalem, known as Hiruhārama to Māori, was on the boundary between the upriver area controlled by the Hau Hau and a downriver district in which local Māori were more friendly to the colonial regime and the missionaries.

At one time, the conflict actually came to Jerusalem in the form of a short battle on nearby Moutoa Island the 14th of May 1864, the one commemorated in Whanganui's Moutoa Gardens, at Pākaitore.

Up the river, you can see still-standing niu poles erected by the Hau Hau: wooden poles that have a vertical staff and four cross members pointing to the four winds, spiritual antennae intended to radiate the spirit of war to all points of the compass.

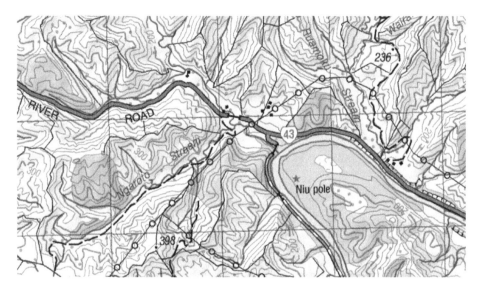

A section of the upper Waikato River shown the location of a Niu pole. Map data by LINZ via NZ Topo Map, 2020.

One of these is the Riri Kore pole, erected when the Hau Hau decided to fight no more. Riri Kore means 'No Anger' or 'No Battle'. This pole was intended to radiate the spirit of peace, and thus cancel the others out.

According to the web page text by the late historian Judith Binney, as of the time of this chapter's preparation,

"These 'niu' (news) poles stand at Maraekōwhai reserve along the Whanganui River. Niu poles were raised by adherents of the Pai Mārire faith

356

and were used in religious rituals. The pole called Rongo Niu (long pole, according to James Cowan) was erected in 1864 during the New Zealand wars. Hauhau warriors carried out final rituals at this niu pole before departing for the battle of Moutoa. The pole called Riri Kore (no war) was erected at the end of the war in recognition of peace."

(James Cowan was a historian remembered mainly for a two-volume work called *The New Zealand Wars: a history of the Maori campaigns and the pioneering period,* first published in the 1920s and re-issued in the 1950s.)

I've mentioned how the <u>Ringatū</u> sect, meaning upraised hand, was founded by Te Kooti on the east coast of the North Island. Actually, Te Kooti drew his inspiration from the Pai Mārire founder, <u>Te Ua Haumēne</u>, who used this gesture.

Te Ua Haumēne, from James Cowan, 'The New Zealand Wars', Vol 2 (1922), via Wikimedia Commons. Public domain image.

Oh, and there's one last thing. In the 1960s, there were plans to dam the Whanganui River with a 165 metre (540 feet) high dam and submerge its scenic banks all the way from Ātene, which is only about thirty kilometres from Whanganui by road, all the way up to Taumarunui. This ultimately never happened.–. fortunately. Instead, waters were taken from the headwaters of the Whanganui for the Tongariro Power Scheme, to wind up in Lake Taupō, which is part of the Waikato River system. As such the Whanganui River now runs starved of water, and this contributes to its greening and pollution as well. I have a blog post which talks about this and also about Ātene, an extraordinary place in its own right. It's linked just below, along with a post on which the rest of this chapter is based.

Blog posts with more images:

a-maverick.com/blog/tales-of-the-whanganui-rediscovering-the-rhine-of-new-zealand

a-maverick.com/blog/the-remarkable-dry-river-at-atene

CHAPTER THIRTY-SIX

Te Araroa

THE WORD Araroa translates from Māori to English as 'long pathway' and it is just that. Many of the attractions of this book are on, or close to, Te Araroa, the long pathway. This is a continuous, three-thousand-kilometre walking track stretching from Cape Rēinga in the North to Bluff in the South (the pathway does not officially extend to Stewart Island/Rakiura, south of the South Island, but does so unofficially.) Along the way, it explores New Zealand's diverse environment with its plains, volcanoes, mountains, rivers, lakes and valleys.

Te Araroa, the Long Pathway. *Sketched from official sources.*

Te Araroa provides some of the best of New Zealand's tramping experiences. Many of the trail sections are also great day or two-day walks. Overall, Te Araroa is a very different trail from the traditional backcountry tracks that stick exclusively to the hills, as it connects settlements, townships and cities. Te Araroa is routed in such a way that trampers can be a benefit to the local communities by paying for experiences such as marae stays and other cultural experiences, or by buying food and paying for accommodation. The trail is designed to provide a wide variety of New Zealand experiences to locals as well as foreign visitors.

The Te Araroa trail has quite a history, with the idea of a walk stretching the length of the country being first discussed in Auckland in the late 1960s. In 1975, the New Zealand Walkways Commission was set up with a mandate to form a 'scenic trail' based on the Pennine Way in the United Kingdom but found it too difficult. DOC tried again in 1995 and made it one of its goals in its Walkways Policy. DOC also proposed giving high priority to a network of countryside tracks crossing private land, as in the United Kingdom.

Today, an organisation called the Te Araroa Trust has at last achieved and indeed surpassed the goal of the great walkway, first set in the 1960s, with this beautiful trail: an achievement that has also expanded the range of accessible locations to tramp. Besides the trust, and the local authorities, there are also many volunteers who have helped to realise this remarkable goal.

> The website of the Te Araroa Trust is **teararoa.org.nz**.

There is just one major problem still to be solved, and that is the excessive amount of Te Araroa that actually consists of walking or bicycling along main roads, excessively close to speeding traffic. If this issue can be overcome, New Zealand will have a long trail it really can be proud of.

Conclusion

WRITING this book has made me realise just how much more of New Zealand I need to see. And ironically enough this includes the island where most New Zealanders live, the North Island, which is nevertheless regarded as 'the other island' in tourism and travel terms even by New Zealanders themselves, let alone by those who arrive at Auckland International Airport and immediately jet on to Queenstown, if they don't land there directly, as you can do from Australia (in normal times, at any rate).

As I mentioned in the Introduction, some of the material in this book was covered in my earlier book *A Maverick New Zealand Way*. It was only after that book came out that I felt I'd short-changed the North Island a bit myself, writing extensively about adventures in the South Island's mountains and beside its lakes, and decided I had to redress the balance.

I certainly feel privileged to have done what I have done, with all its trials and tribulations. It is important to escape immediate pressures, to 'contemplate the sublime' as philosophers say, and get back to what really matters in life. We also learn to appreciate just what a landscape we are blessed with.

That goes, of course, for the inhabitants of most countries, which have their natural attractions. But I like to think that it applies doubly in beautiful New Zealand, both North and South.

Furthermore, unless we learn to appreciate our nature and protect it, it may not be there forever.

Acknowledgements and Thanks

I would like to thank my friends and family – you know who you are – and the many people I have met along the way.

I would like to thank my editor Chris Harris, and once more to thank Nicki Botica Williams for sharing her photos of Auckland's wild western shore and streams.

Any further errors or omissions that remain are, of course, all mine.

Other books by Mary Jane Walker

Did you like *The Neglected North Island?* If so, please leave a review! You may also like to have a look at one of the other books I've written, which all have sales links on my website <u>a-maverick.com</u>.

A Maverick Traveller

A funny, interesting compilation of Mary Jane's adventures. Starting from her beginnings in travel it follows her through a life filled with exploration of cultures, mountains, histories and more.

A Maverick New Zealand Way

The forerunner of the present book, A Maverick New Zealand Way was a finalist in Travel at the International Book Awards, 2018.

A Maverick Cuban Way

Trek with Mary Jane to Fidel's revolutionary hideout in the Sierra Maestra. See where the world nearly ended and the Bay of Pigs and have coffee looking at the American Guantánamo Base, all the while doing a salsa to the Buena Vista Social Club.

A Maverick Pilgrim Way

Pilgrim trails are not just for the religious! Follow the winding ancient roads of pilgrims across the continent of Europe and the Mediterranean.

A Maverick USA Way

Mary Jane took Amtrak trains around America and visited Glacier, Yellowstone, Grand Teton, Rocky Mountain and Yosemite National Parks before the snow hit. She loved Detroit which is going back to being a park, and Galveston and Birmingham, Alabama.

A Maverick Himalayan Way

Mary Jane walked for ninety days and nights throughout the Himalayan region and Nepal, a part of the world loaded with adventures and discoveries of culture, the people, their religions and the beautiful landscapes.

A Maverick Inuit Way and the Vikings

Mary Jane's adventures in the Arctic take her dog sledding in Greenland, exploring glaciers and icebergs in Iceland, and meeting some interesting locals.

Iran: Make Love not War

Iran is not what you think. It's diverse, culturally rich, and women have more freedoms than you would imagine.

The Scottish Isles: Shetlands, Orkneys and Hebrides (Part 1)

In 2018, Mary Jane decided to tour the islands that lie off the coast of Scotland. She made it around the Orkney and Shetland groups, and to the inner-Hebrides islands of Raasay, Mull, Iona and Staffa as well. She was amazed to discover that Norse influences were as strong as Gaelic ones, indeed stronger on the Orkneys and Shetlands.

Catchy Cyprus: Once was the Island of Love

This is a short book based on Mary Jane's visit to Cyprus, the island that copper's named after and the legendary birthplace of Aphrodite, Greek goddess of love. A former British possession in the Mediterranean Sea, Cyprus is divided into Greek-dominated and Turkish-dominated regions with United Nations troops in between.

Lonely Lebanon: A Little Country with a Big History

"I visit the small country of Lebanon, north of Israel, a country whose name means 'the white' in Arabic because of its snow-capped mountains. Lebanon is divided between Christian and Muslim communities and has a history of civil war and invasion. For all that, it is very historic, with lots of character packed into a small space."

Eternal Egypt: My Encounter with an Ancient Land

In this book, Mary Jane explores Egypt, a cradle of civilisation described by the ancient Greek historian Herodotus as the 'gift of the Nile'. Mary Jane put off going to Egypt for years before she finally went. She's glad she did: there's so much more to Egypt than the pyramids!